CONTROLLING

CONTROLLING CRIME

The Classical Perspective
in Criminology

BOB ROSHIER

OPEN UNIVERSITY PRESS
Milton Keynes · Philadelphia

Open University Press
12 Cofferidge Close
Stony Stratford
Milton Keynes MK11 1BY

First Published 1989

British Library Cataloguing in Publication Data

Roshier, Bob
    Controlling crime: the classical perspective
    in criminology.
    1. Criminology. Theories
    I. Title
    364′.01

ISBN 0-335-15874-9
        0-335-15873-0 (paper)

Typeset in Monophoto Ehrhardt by Vision Typesetting, Manchester
Printed in Great Britain by the Alden Press, Oxford

Contents

Preface

The classical conception of human action, with its emphasis on freedom, rationality and choice, has in recent times found new favour with the rise of monetarist economics. It has also been influential in areas outside of economics, including criminology. Like its monetarist relation, the criminological version has tended to be associated with a politically conservative stance. It has focused on effective crime control, assuming humans to be free, rational and choice-making and hence best kept in order by increasing the risks of committing crime. In emphasising deterrence through punishment and the reduction of impunity, it can legitimately claim to be heir to the original classical position, laid down in the eighteenth century.

Yet, in the late 1960s and early 1970s there was a brief flirtation with classical ideas in a rather different context. The interactionist and 'societal reaction' theorists of that time, in their opposition to positivist criminology, resurrected (explicitly in the case of David Matza) the basic classical view of human action. But in this version criminals and deviants were seen as rationally responding to oppressive forces of social definition and reaction and, in the early 'radical' criminology that grew out of it, as being 'free' to fight back against these forces.

Since then, the radical impulse behind the resurrection of classicism seems to have become dissipated. All that is now left is the intensely practical concern with crime control through street-level crime-prevention programmes. While not denying the realism of this current focus, the aim of this book is to return to the wider context in which classical ideas were beginning to be explored in the 1960s and 1970s.

In Part One the foundations and subsequent fate of classical ideas are explored. The focus is on their persistence and continuity as well as the opposition they have generated. But above all, the emphasis is on their undeveloped potential. Part Two is an attempt to develop that potential into a 'postclassical' perspective which can help to make sense of many of the findings, and help resolve some of the contradictions, of criminological research into crime and its control.

In both parts much ground is covered in few pages. This has meant that I have not attempted to be, and do not claim to have been, at all comprehensive in the coverage of the many issues and vast literature that relate to the areas I have encountered. Rather, I have been highly selective, concentrating on the points that bear most directly on the argument that I have attempted to develop. In other words, breadth of coverage has been sacrificed in the interest, I hope, of continuity of argument.

Classical Criminology

Introduction

For nearly a hundred years – from the last quarter of the nineteenth century to the 1960s – classical criminology was treated as a humane, well-intentioned, but essentially misguided ancestor of criminology 'proper'. During that period, those writers of criminology textbooks who thought it worthwhile to include the classical school usually relegated it to a special and rather inferior category: thus Vold (1958, p. 14), one of the most widely quoted who did include it, dubbed it 'Administrative and Legal Criminology' and as 'essentially pre-scientific in any modern sense of the human behaviour sciences'. For Vold (1958, p. 26) the main virtue that made it worthy of consideration at all in a serious criminology textbook of that period seemed to be that it had given up 'the supernatural as a principle of explanation and as a guide to criminal procedure'.

Vold's assessment, particularly the reference to 'pre-scientific' status, perhaps indicates the reason for the predominantly marginal interest in classical criminology during that time. The bulk of criminology textbooks that were produced then were written from a taken-for-granted positivist standpoint. Their central concern was the 'scientific' study of the causes of crime. Classical criminology, with its old-fashioned view of humans as free-willed, rational and hedonistic, had little or nothing to say about this: we were portrayed as committing crime because, and when, we saw it as being in our interests to do so. The causes of crime were not seen as a problem (though its control was). It is hardly surprising that such views were of little more than historical interest to positivist criminologists. In Vold's characterisation, classical criminology was merely a mid-way stage in the linear historical progress of human intellect from the supernatural to the scientific view of human behaviour.

Since that early edition of Vold's textbook, however, ideas have changed (including those of Vold himself: see Vold and Bernard, 1986, which includes a much less dismissive view of classical criminology than that quoted above). In the 1960s there was an unprecedented reaction against positivism in various branches of the human sciences. The positivist assumption that we are ourselves suitable objects for study with models borrowed from the natural sciences and that we can be changed by applied technology came under special attack, with the criminological version a prime target (as numerous studies have subsequently documented). An early work (Matza, 1964) consciously resurrected classical themes as part of this attack. Such themes have subsequently continued to appear – sometimes recognised as such, sometimes not; the classical perspective is no longer the poor relation that it was.

Part One is an outline and assessment of this birth, death and (partial) rebirth of the classical perspective.

1 Foundations: Beccaria and the Basis of Classicism

Some tangible motives had to be introduced, therefore, to prevent the despotic spirit, which is in every man, from plunging the laws of society into its original chaos. These tangible motives are the punishments established against infractors of laws . . . These motives, by dint of repeated presentation to the mind, counterbalance the powerful impressions of the private passions that oppose the common good (Beccaria, 1963, p. 12).

By far the most significant figure responsible for the formulation of the principles of classical criminology was Cesare Beccaria (1738–94). Indeed, classical criminology is almost entirely constituted by the one, short book that he wrote, *Dei Delitti e delle Pene* in 1764 (Beccaria, 1963). It was not particularly its originality that distinguished it – it consisted mainly of ideas borrowed from the Enlightenment and from earlier social contract writers. Nor, evidently, was Beccaria himself a towering figure of his time; in fact, he was unknown when he wrote it, never wrote anything else of note and was an embarrassing failure in personal appearances to evangelise his cause. It has even been darkly insinuated by Paolucci (in Beccaria, 1963) that he may merely have been used as a front by his radical friends, the Verri brothers, who were too much in trouble with the authorities at the time to risk writing it themselves.

Whatever its origins, *Dei Delitti e delle Pene* is a masterpiece of compression, focusing its borrowed ideas into a comprehensive, coherent treatise on the iniquities of the contemporary European criminal justice systems and offering a systematic alternative. The iniquities that Beccaria had in mind were cruelty, arbitrariness and inefficiency (like all reformers he has, of course, been accused of gross exaggeration – see Paolucci in Beccaria, 1963); the alternatives he offered were humanity, consistency and rationality.

Cesare Beccaria: *On Crimes and Punishments*

Beccaria starts by looking at the justification of the right to punish; he concludes that it is to be found in the social contract whose central tenet he declares to be 'the greatest happiness of the greatest number' (it is possible that he is responsible for originating this particular cliché). The social contract involves our sacrificing a portion of our personal liberty to achieve this end, but *not* out of some innate desire for the common good, since 'If it were possible, every one of us would prefer that the compacts binding others do not bind us'. Rather, it is because, 'Weary of living in a continual state of war, and of enjoying liberty rendered useless by the uncertainty of preserving it, [we] sacrifice a part so that [we] might enjoy the rest of it in peace and safety' (p. 11).[1]

So the social contract is selfishly motivated; it comes about through our rational ability to perceive a personal advantage from it. Consequently, it is precarious. Disincentives are also needed (to 'prevent reversion') in the form of punishments for law infractors. We would will this as part of the social contract because our own selfishness would enable us to see its necessity.

Punishments, however, must not exceed the minimum that is necessary to deter – we would not, Beccaria again argues, will it otherwise in the social contract. Thus, the 'humanitarianism' that informs his programme is also derived from selfish, rational motives; it stems from the fact that, since we can imagine ourselves breaking the contract, we can also imagine ourselves being the objects of punishment.

Beccaria's reputation for humanity comes from the famous sections that oppose the use of torture and of capital punishment. While his arguments about capital punishment are still of great relevance, it now seems rather odd that it could have been thought necessary to have to argue against the use of torture for extracting confessions. At the time Beccaria was writing, however, it was assumed that God and righteousness would prevent innocents from breaking under torture and falsely confessing. He points to the irrationality of this assumption and makes the seemingly rather obvious point that 'Torture . . . is an infallible means for absolving robust scoundrels and for condemning innocent persons who happen to be weak' (p. 32).

His opposition to capital punishment is, again, based on utilitarian and social contractual reasons. No rational person, he says, would enter into a social contract that would 'leave to other men the choice of killing him'. His alternative, 'perpetual servitude', is chosen because of its supposed greater effectiveness as a general deterrent rather than its lesser cruelty:

> To anyone raising the argument that perpetual servitude is as painful as death and therefore equally cruel, I will reply that, adding up all the moments of unhappiness of servitude, it may well be even more cruel; but these are drawn out over an entire lifetime, while the pain of death exerts its whole force in a moment. And precisely this is the advantage of penal servitude, that it inspires terror in the spectator more than in the sufferer (p. 48).

Beccaria was not, on the other hand, opposed to corporal punishment. This is much less often commented upon, probably because he mentions it in a rather throwaway fashion, losing it in a section almost entirely devoted to the argument that noblemen should receive the same punishments as people of the lower orders. For crimes which are 'attempts against the person' he says, 'the penalties . . . should always be corporal punishments' (p. 68). That is absolutely all he has to say on the matter. I shall return to the question of Beccaria's humanity later.

As the above quotation on 'perpetual servitude' suggests, Beccaria considered the purpose of punishment to be to deter, with the emphasis on general rather than individual deterrence. It is aimed at minds rather than bodies (though it uses bodies) and its *intent* is not to torment (though it may do so). Its overriding concern is with efficient crime control. Although this is quite different from retribution (an aim that Baccaria specifically rejects), he retains the idea, usually associated with retribution, that the punishment should be *proportional* to the crime – but not, he insists, proportional to its *sinfulness* (since only God can gauge that). It should, instead, be proportional to the *harm done to society*. All personal characteristics of offenders, including their subjective intent, should be excluded from consideration; the sole measure of the punishment should be the objective harm done. If we ask who is to gauge that (presumably not God), he gives the unhelpful and not a little pompous reply that it is 'known with clarity and precision only by some few thinking men in every nation and every age' (p. 64).

The reason that Beccaria gives for his requirement of proportionality is that 'If an equal punishment be ordained for two crimes that do not equally injure society, men will not be any more deterred from committing the greater crime, if they find a greater advantage associated with it' (p. 63). It is this feature of Beccaria's programme that has caused more problems than probably anything else, as we shall see later. Briefly, the problems are both practical and moral. On the practical side, Beccaria makes the quite unwarranted assumption that more serious crimes are more attractive and of necessity require more serious punishments to deter them than do lesser ones. The moral problem arises from Beccaria's insistence that all personal characteristics of offenders and circumstances of their offences should be excluded from consideration in determining punishments. This violates such deep-seated feelings of justice that it has proved to be unacceptable under any criminal law jurisdiction.

Two other requirements that Beccaria makes of punishments for them to be effective are that they should be *prompt* and *certain*. These two qualities make 'so much stronger and more lasting in the human mind . . . the association of these two ideas *crime* and *punishment*. . . . The association of ideas is the cement that forms the fabric of the human intellect' (p. 56). He attaches great importance to 'the association of ideas' and sees it as being most powerfully achieved where the punishment symbolises the offence as far as possible. Thus property offences should be dealt with by fines (to be earned by forced labour if the offender cannot pay) and violent offences by corporal punishment. Imprisonment, because of its invisibility (symbolism obviously requires public visibility) seems to be relegated to a relatively minor role, though he is not very clear on this. His opposition to capital punishment, on the other hand, does not seem to fit very well with the principle of symbolic representation – the public execution of murderers appears to satisfy all his requirements.

Beccaria concludes with a section on prevention, which he sees as being very much preferable to punishment – it increases aggregate utility, the happiness of the greatest number (or, rather, decreases their aggregate unhappiness). Prevention requires laws to be clear, simple and universally supported. It also seems to require a restriction of the scope of the criminal law and a readiness to consider decriminalisation:

> For one motive that drives men to commit a real crime there are a thousand that drives them to commit those indifferent acts which are called crimes by bad laws; and if the probability of crimes is proportionate to the number of motives, to enlarge the sphere of crimes is to increase the probability of their being committed (p. 94).

Another important resource for the prevention of crime is the spread of enlightenment via education. 'Knowledge' says Beccaria 'breeds evil in reverse ratio to its diffusion' since 'no enlightened person can fail to approve the clear and useful public compacts of mutual security' which constitute the social contract (p. 95). Beccaria summarises his arguments in a 'general theorem':

> In order for punishment not to be, in every instance, an act of violence of one or of many against a private citizen, it must be essentially public, prompt, necessary, the least possible in the given circumstances, proportionate to the crimes, dictated by the laws (p. 99).

Beccaria and Bentham: Utility and Humanity

In Britain, the ideas of Beccaria are probably best known through their influence on Bentham. Certainly, Bentham acknowledged his debt to Beccaria. Almost all of the basic principles of his utilitarian programme in relation to the criminal justice system can be traced back to *Dei Delitti e delle Pene*. The most striking difference between them is in the amount they wrote – Beccaria so little and Bentham so much. If Beccaria's fault was brevity, then Bentham's was immense, often boring, detail (as exhibited, for example, in his celebrated attempt to specify all possible pains and pleasures).

One important distinction between the two writers is that Bentham became much more favourably disposed towards the prison as a medium of criminal reformation than Beccaria appeared to be (a point to which I shall return later). Hart (1983, p. 51) has drawn attention to a second important difference: Beccaria, he says, has 'a respect for the individual person' that is lacking in Bentham:

> I think that very often where Bentham and Beccaria differ in detail this is traceable to Beccaria's conviction that what may be done in the name of utility should be limited by consideration of what befits the dignity of man.

In that long-noted contradiction between the happiness of the greatest number and the 'natural' rights of the individual, Hart locates the two writers in quite different positions. This is an important distinction, since it relates to a fundamental dilemma in the classical conception of what is legitimate in punishing crime.

Clearly, what humanity there is in Bentham is very much aggregate humanity;

his willingness to sacrifice individual humanity to achieve it is legendary. A good example (and one that affords an interesting comparison with Beccaria) is his attitude towards torture. Bentham was perfectly willing to countenance torture if it would reveal information that would prevent more injury and suffering than was used in obtaining it (Twining and Twining, 1973). Beccaria, as already noted, was famous for his opposition to torture. Tempting as this comparison is, however, it is not quite fair; they were talking about different things. Beccaria was opposing the use of torture for extracting confessions. His opposition was on utilitarian rather than humane grounds: it does not work; it 'absolves robust scoundrels' and condemns week innocents. Indeed, Beccaria always avoided direct appeals to humanity or individual rights. Even in his opposition to capital punishment, as we have seen, his arguments are in terms of effectiveness and utility. He was not at all put off by the possibility that his alternative 'may well be even more cruel'. Nor was he averse to corporal punishments where the logic of his 'symbolic representation' thesis seemed to require it. Indeed, the logic seemed to require that such punishment should take place in public. Since it would have been unlikely that many property offenders would have been able to pay the fines that he advocated, they would mostly have been subjected to the forced labour that he proposed as the alternative. None of these examples suggests a particularly marked concern with the 'dignity of man'.

Beccaria's appearance of humanity is perhaps to some extent due to the fact that, unlike Bentham, he often glossed over the darker implications of his arguments. This, in turn, suggests that perhaps he found himself in a dilemma – caught between his naturally humane feelings and the logic of his unsentimental, utilitarian theory. Yet, on the other hand, his particular version of the social contract *allows* for both. The requirement of effective deterrence is potentially extremely harsh. It is moderated by the fact that since we are all naturally deviant given the chance, we can identify with offenders because we can imagine them being ourselves. This is why only the minimum necessary punishments are prescribed; we would not will it otherwise. The view that the punishments are, potentially, things that may happen to us provides a selfish (and, therefore, suitably utilitarian) basis for a concern with humanity and the rights of the individual offender. Becarria uses just such an argument against capital punishment (in addition to his rational, effectiveness arguments); we simply would not enter into a social contract that gave someone the right to kill us. What is perhaps surprising, if it *is* the case that Beccaria was moved by humane sentiments towards the individual offender, is that he did not use this argument more often. Would we, for example, be happy with giving someone the right to administer corporal punishment to us (in public)? It seems that Beccaria did not often err, in his balancing of contradictory requirements, in favour of the rights of the individual against the achievement of effective deterrence via symbolic representation.

Whatever Beccaria's personal position, his vision of a social contract set up by people who can at least imagine themselves as the recipients of its punishments is in marked contrast to the later, positivist position that tended to see criminals as different kinds of people altogether. Ferri (1967, p. 7), in his criticisms of classical criminology and its influence, writing in 1917, was particularly concerned with its 'excessive solicitude for delinquents'. The vision of delinquents as a different species of being threatening society provided a potentially much more unfettered entitlement to take action against them than was allowable under Beccaria's version of the social contract that underpinned the classical theory.

Neoclassicism

Beccaria's classical criminology is universally attributed with a powerful influence over subsequent developments in the criminal justice systems of most European countries. Paolucci claims (in Beccaria 1963, p. ix) that *Dei Delitti e delle Pene* has had 'more practical effect than any other treatise ever written in the long campaign against barbarism in criminal law and procedure'. And Monachesi (1960, p. 49) goes as far as to say that 'The reader will find proposed in his essay practically all of the important reforms in the administration of criminal justice and in penology which have been achieved in the civilised world since 1764'.

An abbreviated version of the 'general theorem' with which Beccaria summarised his arguments was incorporated as Article VIII of the 'Declaration of the Rights of Man and of the Citizen', passed by the revolutionary National Assembly of France, on 26 August 1789. However, actual attempts to legislate and operate Beccaria's programme in Europe encountered a serious stumbling block, and the final outcome was invariably something significantly different from what he actually proposed. The main example was the French Code of 1791, where legislators consciously attempted to put his ideas into practice. The problem that soon emerged was Beccaria's insistence on the strict proportionality between offences and punishments, regardless of the circumstances of the offence or characteristics of the offender. This proved to be quite unacceptable, and the French Code moved progressively over the years towards allowing judges more and more discretion to vary punishments on precisely these grounds. The resulting system has come to be referred to as 'neoclassicism' – a retention of the assumption of free will, but with an allowance that it is sometimes freer than at other times and that the proportionality of punishments should be adjusted to these varying degrees of freedom. Neoclassicism, in this sense, became the basis of all European and Western criminal law jurisdictions and has remained so, more or less, to this day.

Even in Britain, with its relative isolation from, and suspicion of, continental legal thinking, Beccaria's ideas made some impression. In 1833 commissioners were appointed to rationalise the criminal law and procedure. Radzinowicz and Hood (1986, p. 726) have noted their obvious (and acknowledged) debt to Beccaria. But these ideas soon became diluted (very much along 'neoclassical' lines), 'Perhaps because of the English Common Law tradition that room should always be left to accommodate the peculiarities of individual cases' (ibid., p. 727). Eventually, however, the whole project came to nothing. Any idea of codification was out of keeping with the English tradition of relatively unfettered judicial discretion and the elasticity of the common law. But despite this, the English system developed to incorporate 'neoclassical' assumptions very similar to those on the Continent.

The main individual characteristics that have been incorporated, under neoclassicism, as making a difference to the culpability of offenders have been age, mental capacity and intent (for instance, degree of premeditation). The reason for their inclusion is that they are seen as influencing (or being indicative of) the responsibility of offenders for their actions. They are expressive of the sentiments of retributive justice that Beccaria wished to exclude from consideration of punishments. He was solely concerned with whether punishments were effective as deterrents and not with whether they were 'fair' (though, as we shall see later, his views on deterrence were also problematic). Indeed, his insistence that punishments should only reflect the harm done to society and have nothing to do with subjective intent would seem to imply that the accident-prone should be treated the same as those who cause harm by design! Perhaps not surprisingly, no criminal justice system was able to take on such gross violations of widely-held sentiments of retributive justice.

Interestingly, although neoclassicism allowed individual differences to influence punishments on the grounds of justice, in doing so it paved the way for the later, positivist conception of the causes and treatment of crime. For in accepting that age and, more importantly, insanity could influence the degree of individuals' responsibility for their actions it was also accepting that in some cases, and to some extent at least, human actions could be seen as *determined*. Thus, it began to incorporate the principles of determinism and the differentiation of offenders from non-offenders that were to be the later hallmarks of positivist criminology.

Classicism and the Prison

Neoclassicism represented, at least in part, a conscious attempt by reformers to put into practice Beccaria's ideas about the administration of criminal justice. On the other hand, the relationship between classical criminology and the major development in *penal* practice in the ensuing century – the rising dominance of the prison – is much more problematic. When I say 'relationship' I mean this in its purely formal sense; there is no attempt here to make any claim about possible causal relationships between ideas and practice.[2] But the formal relationship between classical criminology and the prison is of considerable importance since, it has been claimed, they embodied quite different ideas about the way to control crime. The most important exponent of this view has been Michel Foucault (1977). He claims that by the latter half of the eighteenth century the fading 'monarchical law' of the *ancien régime* was being confronted by two different alternatives: the programme of the 'reforming jurists' (classical criminology) and that of the advocates of the prison:

> Broadly speaking, one might say that, in monarchical law, punishment is a ceremonial of sovereignty; it uses the ritual marks of the vengeance that it applies

to the body of the condemned man; and it deploys before the eyes of the spectators an effect of terror as intense as it is discontinuous, irregular and always above its own laws, the physical presence of the sovereign and of his power. The reforming jurists, on the other hand, saw punishment as a procedure for requalifying individuals as subjects, as juridical subjects; it uses not marks, but signs, coded sets of representations, which would be given the most rapid circulation and the most general acceptance possible by citizens witnessing the scene of punishment. Lastly, in the project for a prison institution that was then developing, punishment was seen as a technique for the coercion of individuals; it operated methods of training the body – not signs – by the traces it leaves, in the form of habits, in behaviour; and it pressupposed the setting up of a specific power for the administration of the penalty (ibid., p. 130–1).

It was the prison, of course, which was to come out on top. Indeed, Beccaria's classical model, at least as far as the form and content of actual penal treatments are concerned, has never really been tried – if we are to accept Foucault's version of events.

There are two elements in Foucault's characterisation of the prison as an alternative model to that of classicism. First, there is the prison itself, as a physical entity – apparently given only a very minor role in the classical model. Second, there is the *aim* – the prison (according to Foucault), being concerned with transforming individual offenders into non-offenders via disciplinary training, classicism with utilising individual offenders to symbolise the offence and deter others. I think there is evidence to suggest that neither of these distinctions was, in practice, nearly as sharp as Foucault suggests.

To take the second element first, it does seem to be true that there is not much mention in Beccaria's book of reformative effects on the individual offender; he is far more concerned with frightening off potential offenders. Even where he does show an interest in 'education' it is, as we have seen, only as a preventive device aimed at the public at large. However, this does not mean that his position was incompatible with individual reformation; he just did not happen to consider it. Bentham, starting from almost identical premises as Beccaria, gets much nearer to it. Ignatieff (1978) suggests that Bentham like the prison reformer John Howard, also arrived at the idea of the corrigibility of man by re-education directed at the mind, albeit it by a different route. Bentham arrived at it via his belief in the universality of reason and hence the possibility of correctly socialising man's instinct for pleasure; Howard by his belief in original sin, guilt and the possibility of awakening man's consciousness of sin.

Anyway, whatever the ideas that inspired the advocates of the prison, it would obviously be very dangerous to assume that their ideas were automatically embodied in the actual operation of the prison system when it came into being. Garland (1985b), in his detailed consideration of the Victorian prison system, concluded that, for Britain at least, Foucault's characterisation is wide of the mark. Individualised reformation as a dominant penal principle did not emerge here until the early part of the twentieth century, when positivist criminology was in the ascendant (though, again, that is not to suggest a simple causal relation). Garland puts Foucault as being around a century out in his characterisation! His analysis (Garland 1985b, p. 32) concludes that 'the constraints of legal principle and political ideology' produced a system aimed at 'uniformity, equality of treatment and proportionality' in which concerns for individual reformation played only a very minor part. Thus Garland's version of the prison suggests the mixture of Beccarian classicism (proportionality for deterrent purposes) and retributive justice (proportionality according to desert) that, as we have seen, was the hallmark of neoclassicism. Foucault, of course, acknowledged that the reformative ideals that gave rise to the prison were a failure, in practice, from the start. Garland, however, seems to go rather further than this in suggesting that, in Britain at least, the emergent prison system never really embodied a 'reformative' alternative to classicism and neoclassicism at all.

The other distinction that Foucault makes relates to the significance of the institution of the prison itself. Again, at first reading, the evidence appears to be on his side: there is scarcely a mention of the prison in Beccaria's book. However, as we have seen earlier in relation to corporal punishment, it is instructive to look at the 'small print' in his writings. Beccaria's prescribed punishment for property crime was the fine. He recognised, however, that since most property crime was committed by the poor, they would not be able to pay fines. Consequently, they were to be subjected to forced labour to pay the equivalent. Let us examine the implications of this; property crime became by far the most common form of crime during the period in which the prison emerged; therefore forced labour would have become the most common punishment; forced labour requires incarceration (people tend not to turn up for it of their own free will). Would Beccaria's programme have looked much different in practice? The only real difference would have been that since Beccaria required his punishments to be public, his offenders would have laboured in the open air during the day rather than within the confines of their prison (presumably led out in chain-gangs). Even the particular architectural form of the prison, with its emphasis on facilitating supervision, discipline and hygiene, was hardly alien to the spirit of rationality and efficiency that inspired classicism. It was, after all, Bentham's 'panopticon' that provided the inspirational model.

It is true that Beccaria's classical programme has never been given a full trial (the image of his public floggings and toiling chain-gangs rather than his denial of capital punishment may help the liberal-minded to feel this less of a loss). But despite this, the prison does not appear to represent the radically different model that Foucault suggests. Rather, it seems that, in its usage at least, it can best be seen as having been incorporated into the neoclassical compromise which has dominated most Western criminal justice systems.

Conclusions: The Basis of Classicism

Beccaria's classical programme is a mixture of basic assumptions about the nature of human beings and the way they relate to crime and conformity, and empirical conclusions that he draws from these assumptions about how best to control crime.

It is the former that constitute the 'classical perspective' and, in this final section, I want to try and extricate them and look at some of the problems that Beccaria's version of them encountered. In doing so I am not suggesting that I am delineating some objective essence of classicism. What follows is, of course, a personal selection.

I think the classical perspective can be seen as incorporating three fundamental assumptions about the nature of human beings that are crucial to it position on crime and conformity: *freedom, rationality* and *manipulability.*

Freedom

Like those who advocate retributive justice, Beccaria sees humans as free-willed and choice-making. It is important, however, to distinguish his use of the conception of human freedom. Under retributive justice punishment is justified because it is 'deserved' by free, choice-making individuals who are held responsible for their actions. As we have seen, Beccaria's justification for punishment was on quite different, purely utilitarian grounds: efficient crime control. His utilitarianism required a practical, socially useful justification for punishment; retribution was totally inadequate. A bonus of rejecting retribution, it seemed, was that he could avoid the particularly tricky problems raised in trying to assess subjective intent, desert and responsibility.

Perhaps Beccaria was also conscious of the incompatibility of retribution and deterrence as penal aims. It is certainly the case that sentencing practice to the present day has manifested an uneasy and uneven relationship between the two. But, as we saw in the discussion of neoclassicism, it was unrealistic to suppose that questions of intent and responsibility could be abandoned. To do so would not only be to abandon deep-seated conceptions of justice and desert, but to abandon the conception of 'guilt' itself. For Beccaria's conception of punishing purely in proportion to harm done failed to distinguish between 'crimes' committed intentionally, under duress or provocation, or even by accident.[3] The sense of injustice created by such a system would inevitably work against its deterrent effectiveness (Beccaria always acknowledged the importance of consent in producing compliance; it is difficult to imagine how his version of the social contract would have allowed such a system to operate).

Beccaria's attempt to avoid considerations of responsibility and desert must be regarded as something of a failure. Later on, positivists attempted to do the same by postulating a view of humans as determined in their actions by forces beyond their control. Whatever one may think of such a position, it at least had the merit of being internally consistent. Beccaria's attempt to avoid the issue while retaining the conception of free will was, perhaps, asking for trouble.

Rationality

According to classical criminology we mostly behave in a rational manner. The goal of our rationality is personal satisfaction; rational self-interest is the key motivational characteristic that governs our relationship with crime and conformity. Since crime, however it is defined in any particular society, always involves some degree of restraint on individual self-interest, our natural tendency is always towards deviation: we will, it seems, always choose the deviant alternative when it suits us and when we think we can get away with it. We appear to be selfish, cynical creatures; our greatest ambition in relation to rules of behaviour is to get other people to obey them so that our own cheating is even more productive.

It is odd that the holder of such a view of human beings could have appeared in history as a humanitarian and heroic opponent of cruelty and barbarism; it seems more appropriate to Hitler than to Beccaria. I have suggested earlier that part of Beccaria's reputation may have resulted from his glossing over the more unsavoury implications of his views, and the fact that his full programme has never really been put into practice; but this is not to deny that, in so far as he has been an influence, he has been a relatively benign one.

A more complex view of our selfishness emerges if we consider its crucial feature – its rationality – a little further. As we have seen, it is our rationality that enables us also to appreciate the personal advantages we would derive from a social contract that promotes self-denial and individual rights. Thus, we are simultaneously capable of altruism. True, it is an altruism grounded in selfishness, but that need not bother us (it can only lead into the usual teenage casuistry about altruism always being ultimately selfish). More important is the fact that our simultaneous selfish demands make it a precarious, situational altruism. It is this ambiguous, contradictory and fluctuating view of our relationship with deviance and conformity that makes the classical position so much more dynamic and plausible than subsequent versions.

Beccaria also implies that our rationality would enable us to agree on what constitutes social harm. It thus provides the basis for defining objective legal rules. In practice though, as we saw, Beccaria thought that most people had not developed their rational insight sufficiently for this to be the case – full rational insight had only been achieved by 'some few thinking men in every nation in every age'. The source of objective legal rules thus appears to be the fully developed rationality of the intellectual elites of different nations. But the implication is that through education we all have the potential to achieve the rational insight of the 'few thinking men' and that, if we did, we, too, would agree on the legal rules that would prevent social harm. Fully rational reasoning, then, would provide an objective, consensual determination of legal rules (though not, of course, any guarantee that we would not break them!).

Despite the possibility of there being objective legal rules, however, Beccaria was clearly not implying that existing legal systems, including that of his own society, necessarily embody them. His critique was open to the inclusion of the *content* as well as the administration of the law. There was certainly no implication in classical criminology, as there was to be in positivist, that we can ignore the content and operation of legal rules in addressing ourselves to the question of the causes and treatment of crime. If anything it is more open to criticism for *solely* addressing itself to these areas.

Manipulability

Although classical criminology clearly portrays humans as being free, responsible and choice-making, this does not preclude their being manipulated. The universally-shared human motive of rational self-interest makes human action predictable, generalisable and controllable. In its concern with manipulation, classical criminology was fully compatible with its successor, positivist criminology; they were both based on the belief that the primary purpose of the penal system was to control crime. However, their views on the way in which this could be achieved were quite different. In the classical version, we are manipulable only through threats or appeals; in the positivist it is through the alteration of mechanistic causal variables.

Beccaria's unwillingness to allow individual differences – whether in terms of personal characteristics or socio-economic position – to enter into considerations of punishment, also distanced him from the positivist version of human manipulability. Strangely enough, as we saw earlier, neoclassicism's inclusion of apparently incompatible retributive concerns provided a more direct link in this respect. Neoclassicism allowed that some offenders were less guilty than others because they were less responsible. When immaturity and, more especially, insanity came to be accepted as making people less responsible, this allowed for the possibility that, for some offenders at least, personal characteristics (or defects) could be seen as both differentiating them from other people and *causing* their criminality. This was to be precisely the starting assumption of positivist criminologists (although they were interested in these differences not because they justified different levels of desert, but because they suggested different types of treatment). To some extent, positivist criminology can be seen as incorporating both the classical concern with rational crime control, and the neoclassical concern with individual differentiation.

In general, the classical perspective contained a peculiarly narrow view of what it actually is that controls human behaviour. It was concerned solely with the formal legal apparatus and relied on a very specific mechanism of control (deterrence by making punishments proportional to crimes). I will be considering the empirical evidence on the effectivness of this particular mechanism in Chapter 9. It has already been noted, however, that there is no particular reason inherent in the classical view of human motivation to assume that this is the only possible means of control. Beccaria just happened to think it was.

There was no consideration at all given to the possibility of disincentives operating in the informal social context, and a total neglect of social and economic *incentives* of all kinds. Leftist critics have suggested that this is because *any* consideration of the socio-economic context of crime would have proved an embarrassment to the classical position. Taylor, Walton and Young (1973), for example, argue that it would inevitably have raised unpalatable issues: that there *are* important socio-economic differences between people, and that these are relevant to crime causation; in other words, issues of *differentiation* and *social determinism* (inimical to the classical position) would have demanded attention. They suggest that the particular problem that confronted Beccaria was the observable fact that criminals were in one important respect clearly differentiated: they were mostly poor. This suggested poverty as both a cause and a rational reason for crime. They give (ibid., pp. 5–6) an example of how Beccaria deals with this problem (in a discussion of theft):

> He who endeavours to enrich himself with the property of others, should be deprived of part of his own. But this crime, alas! is commonly the effect of misery and despair; the crime of that unhappy part of mankind, to whom the right of exclusive property (a terrible and perhaps unnecessary right) has left but a bare existence. Besides, as pecuniary punishments may increase the number of robbers, by increasing the number of poor, and may deprive an innocent family of subsistence, the most proper punishment will be that kind of slavery, which alone can be called just; that is, which makes society, for a time, absolute master of the person, and labour of the criminal, in order to oblige him to repair, by this dependence, the unjust despotism he usurped over the property of another, and his violation of the social compact.

They interpret this as showing that Beccaria, through his commitment to a social contract that accepted the necessity of the inequities and poverty resulting from private property, was forced to overlook these as much more plausible reasons for crime than his own. Interestingly, Paolucci in his translation of Beccaria (1963, p. 74) (not the one used by Taylor, Walton and Young) adds the following footnote to the above passage:

> in a manuscript of Beccaria's own hand as well as in the first edition, Beccaria had written 'a terrible but perhaps necessary right' – that is to say, quite the opposite of 'a terrible and perhaps unnecessary right,' as found here.

The 'original' actually fits Taylor, Walton and Young's argument rather better than the amended version they quote above which implies at least the *possibility* of poverty as a cause of 'rational' crime. Vold and Bernard (1986, p. 29) are critical of Taylor, Walton and Young for not allowing that Beccaria could see crime as being sometimes rational and justified. But they are being rather generous; whatever Beccaria may have privately thought or hinted at, he never developed his position on these matters. At most, it suggests that he lacked the courage of his more radical convictions, rather than being a straightforward conservative. Certainly, his *intellectual* position would not have been jeopardised by such an extension of his arguments. His version of human freedom and motivation could easily have included poverty as a 'rational' reason for crime; and there was no necessary reason for him to equate his social contract with the status quo as far as property relations were concerned (after all, he did not equate it with the status quo in many other respects).

In general, there was nothing inherent in Beccaria's intellectual position to preclude a consideration of the socio-economic context of crime, any more than there was to necessitate his sole concentration on deterrence that was remarked on earlier. Indeed, it is an oddity that he seemed to see the criminal justice system as being the only aspect of the environment that influences individual decisions about whether it is worthwhile to commit crime or not.

Conclusion

A recent assessment of Beccaria has portrayed him as a cautious conservative who successfully redirected enlightenment thinking away from a potentially much more radical path: 'His sudden fame can be attributed to the relief of educated society that it was possible to hold rational "enlightened" views on human behaviour without having to accept radical materialism' (Jenkins, 1984, p. 113). Jenkins argues that enlightenment thinking in Beccaria's time was 'advanced': atheistic and deterministic ideas proposing that humans are determined by their social environment, that morality is relative and that the justification for the existing social order was consequently bogus, were being openly espoused. He uses William Godwin and the Marquis de Sade as examples. Beccaria's offer of a less radical alternative, says Jenkins, had the effect of postponing the positivist revolution for over a century.

It is true that Beccaria seems careful not to offend. The introduction to his book contains a strong denial that he is an atheist, revolutionary or opponent of sovereign rulers. But this is hardly surprising; such things could get you into trouble (his 'promoters', the Verri brothers, were already in trouble). It is also true that most people would look fairly conventional, even today, when compared with de Sade. What is rather more strange is that Jenkins should portray the postponement of the positivist revolution as being an anti-radical step. After all, when it did come it initially avoided these political problems by the simple device of locating the determinants of crime in the individual's make-up (and for that reason the early version of positivism has been a firm favourite with rulers and governments ever since).

Certainly, positivism did also produce social determinist critiques of the existing order. But then, as I have argued earlier, there was nothing in the basic assumptions of classicism that necessarily prevented it from being equally critical. In both classical and positivist criminology, it is the particular way their basic assumptions are interpreted and developed that establishes their political and ideological positions.

Despite all the problems that have been discussed in relation to the basic assumptions of classical criminology, I have emphasised that they have stemmed mostly from the way they were interpreted, and from their underdevelopment. The assumptions themselves have remained more or less intact, and in Part Two I will return to them in developing a 'postclassical' perspective.

Notes

1 In this section, references where only a page number is given are to Beccaria (1963).
2 For a useful summary and critique of arguments about the ideological and material forces behind the emergence of the prison, see Ignatieff (1985).
3 For a definitive discussion of these problems in the context of a more recent, positivist, attempt to abandon questions of the responsibility of criminals, see Kneale (1967).

2 Opposition: Positivist Criminology

In the space of approximately the last quarter of the nineteenth century positivist criminology 'developed from the idiosyncratic concerns of a few individuals into a programme of investigation and social action which attracted support throughout the whole of Europe and North America' (Garland, 1985a). If we interpret its principles in their widest sense, they were to dominate academic thinking about crime and its treatment until the 1960s. Indeed, when the academic discipline of 'criminology' is referred to it is almost invariably taken to mean only positivist criminology in this wider sense, with its extensive research and literature and established (though competing) theories.

There is a considerable number of textbooks which provide a run-through of positivist research findings and theories and it is not the intention to attempt yet another one here.[1] Rather, my aim is to look at the kinds of assumption that informed the various strands of positivist criminology, and at the way they differed from classical assumptions in both theory and practice.

In the previous chapter it was pointed out that both classical and neoclassical criminology had already incorporated some principles that were to be fundamental to positivism: classical criminology had insisted on practical crime control rather than retributive desert as the aim of punishment, and neoclassicism had allowed for the principle at least of 'determinants' of crime. But to the positivists these similarities were purely superficial, since in both cases there was an underlying assumption that was totally unacceptable to them: free will. In their view this had hopelessly inhibited the quest for the causes of crime in the case of classical criminology, and diverted attention away from social defence in the case of the neoclassicists (since the latter were only interested in 'determinants' of crime in so far as they reduced the offender's responsibility). Above all, the new positivists portrayed the existing penal process based on such principles as having failed to provide for the proper defence of society against crime – partly through pre-scientific wrongheadedness, and partly through a misplaced concern with the rights of offenders (Ferri, 1967).

The positivists' rejection of free will was fundamental to their position. They did not portray it simply as a change in philosophical stance, but as an outcome of the advance in scientific psychological knowledge. As Ferri (1967, p. 289), one of the founder-members, put it: 'The positivist physio-psychology has completely destroyed the belief in free choice or moral liberty, in which it demonstrates we should recognize a pure illusion of subjective psychological observation.' Garland (1985a) suggests that it was the advancement in the standing of 'scientific' psychiatry (together with developments in government statistical surveys and data and the provision, by the prison system, of a captive 'laboratory' for criminological research) that favoured the emergence of positivist criminology at this particular time. This, in turn, was part of what was seen at the time as the natural extension of scientific and technological principles from their successful application to the material and animal world to apply to human beings themselves. Humans could no longer be allowed any such privileged, mystical feature as free will to distinguish them.

The replacement of free will with scientific determinism was consequently the crucial starting point for the new positivist criminology. Before looking further at the way this assumption was developed, it would be useful to clear up a confusion that may arise in the use of the category 'positivist criminology'. In textbooks on criminology it has often been used to distinguish the specific school of thought of the original founding fathers of criminology: Lombroso, Garofalo and Ferri. But it has also been argued that the basic features of positivism applied to *all* causal theories of crime, whether biological (as in the case of the founding fathers), psychological or sociological, that were to appear over the next half century or more (Jeffery, 1960; Matza, 1964).

In order to clarify the two uses of 'positivist criminology', it might be helpful to use the term 'biological positivist' to distinguish the founding fathers from the more general category. However, one of the aims of this chapter is to see if there are the significant continuities that have been claimed. To do this, it is first necessary to see if it is possible to agree on what the crucial principles are that characterise both the original biological positivists and the proposed wider category. Fortunately, this does not appear to be too difficult: Garland (1985a), who has provided a pioneer account of the emergence of the biological positivists, would, I think, agree with Jeffery and Matza on the following: *determinism, differentiation* and *pathology*. These three features also appear to distinguish it from classical criminology (although I will reconsider the distinction later).

Determinism, in the more general positivist sense, means that crime is seen as *behaviour* that is *caused* by biological, psychological or social factors, depending on the academic origins of the criminologist concerned. On this view crime does *not* consist of *actions*, rationally chosen by the 'criminal'.

Differentiation refers to the positivist assumption that there is something (preferably measurably) different about criminals; they may be seen as differing from non-criminals in terms of their biological or psychological make-up, or in terms of their values, again according to the academic origins of the criminologist concerned. There may also be sub-categories of criminals committing different types of crime caused by different types of factors.

Pathology means that criminals are not only different from non-criminals, but there is also something 'wrong' with them. Their different make-up or values are not simply variations of the 'normal'.

Before considering how (and how far) these three features are actually manifested in the different positivist theories, there are two other contingent and inter-dependent features that Jeffery (and Matza following him) pick on as of central significance to the positivist programme: the shift of focus from *crime* to the *criminal*, and the quest for a universal, objective category of 'criminal' behaviour.

It was natural that the original biological positivists should focus exclusively on the criminal, since they were committed to the view that the causes of crime were to be found in the individual's biological make-up. But Jeffery (1960, p. 377) goes much further:

> The importance of the Positive School is that it focussed attention on motivation and on the individual criminal. It sought an explanation of crime in the criminal, not in the criminal law. This is true of every theory of criminal behaviour which is discussed in the textbooks today, even though the explanation is in terms of social and group factors rather than in terms of biological factors . . . The emphasis is still upon the individual offender, not the crime.

What Jeffery (and Matza, who quotes Jeffery in support of his own position) are pointing to here is that whatever positivists chose as the causes of crime, even when they were 'external' such as 'social and group' factors, they always excluded the nature and operation of the criminal law from consideration; such things were simply not taken to be implicated in the process of causing criminal behaviour.

Because positivists were seeking general theories of behaviour to explain crime, they also required 'crime' to be a universal, objective category of behaviour. As Jeffery points out, this meant that the *legal* category was unacceptable since it was too obviously variable over different time periods and between different societies. Positivists, of all varieties, have consequently been caught up in an endless quest for a universal, objective but non-legal concept of 'crime'. The original biological positivists mostly settled for Garofalo's concept of 'natural crime' – 'an act that offends the moral sentiments of pity and probity in a community'. Needless to say Jeffery, and many others, have had little difficulty in showing how all such attempts have inevitably boiled down to the arbitrary moral predilections of the criminologists concerned.

The positivist attempt to disengage itself from legal conceptions of crime and the operations of legal processes generally, clearly marked it off from classical criminology. Jeffery (1960, pp. 367–8) draws an interesting conclusion from this, which echoes one of our concerns in the last chapter:

> the positivistic notion of crime is susceptible to corruption in the hands of corrupt political officials. The fact that Ferri became a member of the Fascist movement

in Italy is of concern to those who regard civil liberties as a fundamental aspect of criminal law. Whereas for Beccaria individual rights are supreme, there are no safeguards against abuse of state power in the work of Garofalo and Ferri.

Garland (1985a, p. 129) has made a similar point: although both classical and positivist criminology incorporated a conception of the relationship between the individual and the state, he sees the positivist version as 'moving from a liberal mode to a more authoritarian, interventionist one', at least in the case of the early, biological school. Such arguments perhaps illustrate the extent of the fall from grace to positivist criminology in recent years. Not only, apparently, was it based on a misguided assumption about the nature of human action, but it also stands accused of paving the way for nefarious political ideologies!

Such a contrast between classicism and positivism seems rather generous to Beccaria. As we saw in the last chapter, he, too, believed in the possibility of an objective category of crime which was not necessarily the same as that defined by the existing criminal law, and its source – the reason of the 'few thinking men in every nation' – seems just as elitist and potentially authoritarian. Indeed, as we also saw in the last chapter, one recent writer (Jenkins, 1984) portrays Beccaria's postponement of the positivist revolution as being anti-radical and supportive of existing authoritarian rulers. Perhaps these contradictory interpretations illustrate the dangers, to which I alluded in the earlier discussion, of assuming an automatic association between classicism and positivism and specific political ideologies.

In general, however, classical and positivist criminology were at almost opposite poles in their views of the significance of the criminal law and its operation; for classicism it was virtually everything, for the positivists it was virtually irrelevant. Garland has argued that the reason why the early, biological positivists had the extraordinary ambition of arriving at a theory of the causes of crime where both the theory and the category of behaviour it was explaining had nothing to do with the criminal law, was that they were also engaged in a struggle to assert themselves as a 'new' profession of penal experts against the 'old', legal profession. But, as Jeffery and Matza rightly point out, this exclusion was to characterise all subsequent positivist criminology. It was also, as we shall see later, to prove to be one of its greatest weaknesses.

The Causes of Crime

Having outlined the key features that have been used to distinguish positivist criminology, in its wider sense, it remains to consider the manner in which they have actually been manifested in the different causal theories that have been proposed. What all the theories have in common is the fundamental assumption that criminals are different from non-criminals in that they have a more or less enduring disposition towards the commission of crime and that this disposition is explicable in terms of 'causes'. However, even in this basic assumption, all had to acknowledge a problem: not *all* crime is committed by such people; a proportion has to be attributed to 'ordinary' people acting on a casual or occasional basis, or in response to extraordinary circumstances. Even the 'hardest' determinists, such as the earliest biological positivists had to allow themselves this let–out.

It is in the proposed causal origins of this enduring disposition towards crime that the different theories diverge. Most of them fall into one (or sometimes more) of three categories in this respect: the disposition is seen as being *inherited, acquired* or *invented*. The choice usually (but by no means always) corresponds to whether the theorist concerned was a *physiological psychologist, non-physiological psychologist* or *sociologist*, respectively – which in turn tends to be associated with the causes being located in the *biology, psyche* or *values* of the individual. In the first two cases, this has also usually meant that criminals are seen as being distinguished by biological or psychic features which are identifiable *separately* from the disposition towards crime (although they are causally implicated in it). That is, they are seen as falling into specific biological or psychological (for example, 'personality') categories which include features other than the criminal disposition. This is not usually the case with the third category: here, criminals are seen as being distinguishable *only* by their (pro-crime) values.

I will not be considering 'control' theories here. This is because although they are usually regarded as an important branch of positivist theorising, they also have much in common with the classical tradition. My aim, later, will be to try to bring them even closer together. For this reason, they will be introduced as part of the 'reassessment' of classicism, in Chapter 3.

Inheritance

If the criminal disposition were inherited then, ideally, we would be able to point to a specific chromosome which was invariably associated with criminal behaviour. Needless to say, this has never been the case, although in the 1960s much excitement was temporarily generated by what appeared to be a relationship between the possession of an extra Y chromosome and persistent crime (see Hall Williams, 1982, Chapter 2). This particular example demonstrated a common pitfall of this kind of positivist criminology: even if all the possessors of the chromosomal anomaly had turned out to be persistent criminals (in the event, they did not) then it would still only have been capable of 'explaining' a fraction of 1 per cent of recorded crime, simply because the condition was so rare. It would indeed have defined a biological category of criminals, but as an explanation of crime in general it would have been virtually irrelevant.

Usually, the supposed relationship between inheritance and crime has been inferred from experimental methods designed to distinguish between the effects of heredity and environment. Until fairly recently the most popular technique was to compare the 'concordance rate' of monozygotic (MZ) twins (who have identical inheritance), with that of dizygotic (DZ) twins (who do not). Perhaps the most celebrated user of this method has been Eysenck (1977) in his theory of crime. The method has always been widely criticised, mainly because of its basic assumption that the effects of environment are equally similar for both types of twin. For this and other reasons, more recent approaches, even those favourably disposed to the idea of criminal inheritance, have tended to reject the twin method as unsound and to rely instead on adoption studies (Ellis, 1982). The assumption here is that if inheritance is a factor then adopted children should be more similar, in their criminality, to their biological than to their adopting parents. There has been a fairly consistent finding in such studies that this does tend to be the case.

However, as Jencks (1987) has pointed out, intriguing as the adoption studies findings are, they are of no practical interest unless we know why they arise – and at present we do not. More importantly, such findings are entirely compatible with an *environmental* explanation of crime 'since genes can influence behaviour by influencing the environment' (ibid., p. 34). That is, whatever it is that is inherited may cause crime because it alters the way in which the person who inherits it is treated by others. One of the examples that Jencks uses to make this point is that of IQ. If IQ were entirely inherited (a contentious assumption) and if IQ were related to crime (many studies have found that low IQ is), this would be perfectly compatible with an environmental explanation: it could well be that people with low IQ are treated unfavourably by others and this unfavourable treatment makes them more likely to commit crime.

What Jencks's argument makes clear is that inheritance theories are only of practical value when the inherited characteristic is specified, together with the way in which it actually operates to produce criminal behaviour. Various other studies have, however, attempted to do this; the usual technique has been to suggest that it is a particular psychological characteristic that is inherited and which leads 'naturally' to crime. That is, they tend to be 'crime-prone personality' theories. This description applies, for example, to the founding fathers of positivist criminology, the biological positivists. Lombroso, the originator of this school, is famous for his theory that criminals can be picked out by inherited physical stigmata (cranial deformities, excessive body hair, and so on). But these features were obviously not the 'causes' of crime, they were merely signs that supposedly enabled us to spot criminals. Their causal theory was in terms of 'atavism': that is, criminals were genetic 'throwbacks' to more primitive human forms. The fact that Lombroso's stigmata turned out to be no more common among criminals than among any other section of the community (see Wolfgang, 1960), although often thought to be a refutation of his theory, is in fact not crucial to it. His causal explanation relied on two factors: that primitive humans were all criminals (even in terms of the definitions of crime operating in nineteenth-century Italy!) and that contemporary criminals (or an important section of them) were genetic throwbacks to these primitives. Needless to say, despite Lombroso's commitment to 'science', he did not provide any evidence to support this preposterous assumption, nor could he have done.

But Lombroso laid down the foundations of most of what was to follow in genetic theories of crime. Even the idea that criminals are physically distinguishable has continued to be pursued to the present day (Hartl *et al.*, 1982), although it later took the form of relating types of body build to personality types. Eysenck, for example, incorporated this idea into his theory and he has probably been the most influential proponent of the genetic strand of positivist criminology in recent years. Eysenck claims that criminals tend to rate highly on two personality characteristics – extroversion and neuroticism – both of which he sees as being predominantly inherited. Various features of these personality characteristics relate to crime, the most important being extroversion's association with a resistance to being 'conditioned' out of various forms of behaviour. A notable feature of Eysenck's theory is his starting assumption that we are all 'naturally' criminal, in line with that of classical criminology. However, in his version we are 'normally' conditioned out of this; his theory still contains the positivist assumption that criminals are different from non-criminals (and 'pathological') – in this case through their abnormal resistance to the conditioning process.

Eysenck's theory depends on a high correlation between criminality and particular personality characteristics identified by personality tests. In this respect, it is part of a very broad category of positivist criminology indeed. The quest for identifiable crime-prone personality types has included learning theorists as well as heredity theorists, psychoanalysts ('anti-social' or 'affectionless' personality theories), and studies not concerning themselves with the question of how such types come about. A common instrument is the 'personality inventory', of which the Minnesota multi-phasic personality inventory (MMPI) is an example. Various surveys of such studies, over a long period of time (Schuessler and Cressey, 1950; Hood and Sparks, 1970; Hindelang, 1972; Feldman, 1977) and covering various categorisations (including Eysenck's), have not suggested widespread agreement on clear-cut categories covering significant proportions of offenders, although various relationships have been found. Further doubt has been thrown on such findings when validity tests have been included (Rathus and Siegel, 1980).

An additional problem that has dogged personality theories is that of tautology; if the categories are to mean anything, they must not be identified *only* by the fact that the people who fall into them tend to commit crimes. This sometimes occurs in a disguised form. An example might be the psychoanalytic theory that 'anti-social' behaviour is caused by failure to develop the superego, where the superego is defined as the faculty that inhibits anti-social behaviour. Tautology also appears to occur sometimes in personality inventories where the 'characteristics' can be boiled down to 'attitudes favourable to the commission of crime' (or 'anti-social' acts); that is to say, 'criminals are people who hold pro-crime values'. However, this is not as tautological as it seems, since it implies a relationship between values and action that is problematic, as we shall see later.

All these problems seem to have made the criminal personality difficult to track down. Thus Wilson and Herrnstein (1985), in their generally sympathetic analysis, conclude that there is probably no such thing. However, they suggest that two *personality traits* have emerged as consistently associated: impulsiveness (lack of ability or desire to defer gratification); and undersocialisation (lack of regard for feelings of others). But there is perhaps a more fundamental problem here:

establishing personality traits or types that are related to crime does not constitute an explanation; it is the way such traits and types come about, and how they lead to crime, that provides that. And they come about through inheritance, acquisition or invention. Attempting to describe the outcome of these processes in terms of 'traits' or 'types' does not really seem to help the explanation very much.

Acquisition

If the tendency towards crime is not seen as being already determined at the point of conception through the genes we inherit, then the obvious conclusion is that it must be subsequently acquired in some way. Positivist theories under this latter heading have taken two quite different forms: the acquisition is through the occurrence of some physical damage (or illness); or it is through learning.

The idea that criminality is the outcome of organic disorder or disease goes back at least as far as Lombroso, who associated crime with epilepsy. In his case, of course, such disorders were presumed to be predominantly inherited. Thus mental disorders as causes of crime in fact straddle both acquisition and inheritance, since the origins of such disorders have always been, and continue to be, a subject of intense debate. Either way, however, the issue need not detain us long. Despite popular beliefs and well-publicised particular instances, all serious analysts agree that the association between specific mental disorders (whatever their origin) and crime is extremely limited (see Hall Williams 1982, Chapter 3). Furthermore, if crimes are clearly established as the outcome of mental disorder they are no longer 'crimes'. For unlike other supposed causal determinants of crime, mental disorder has been accepted by most criminal jurisdictions as taking away some of the fundamental elements that constitute an act as a crime. In other words, to the limited extent that mental disorder explains particular crimes, it denies their very status as crimes. Rather than explaining crime, mental disorder redefines it as something else.

Learning theories have been much more important in positivist theorising about the acquisition of criminal tendencies. Sometimes, however, there is a problem in distinguishing 'learning' theories because they can easily become all-embracing. In its widest sense, learning has been taken to mean changes in people's behaviour, knowledge, beliefs, motives, and so on, brought about as a result of their experiences. With such a wide definition, it might be more useful to consider what this leaves out, rather than what it includes – which gets us back to the categories I am working with here: it excludes inheritance and invention.

Distinguishing inheritance from learning is, I think, no problem: the definition of learning, even in its widest sense clearly excludes it (some learning theorists allow inheritance to play a part *as well as* learning but that, of course, is a different point).

Distinguishing invention presents much more of a problem. By invention I mean behaviour, values, beliefs, and so on, that come about through 'internal' processes of thinking and working out rather than through imitating or mechanically responding to external stimuli. The problem is that these internal processes are bound to be *influenced* by the person's experiences; it would be unreasonable to think of them as being entirely autonomous. Also, some learning theorists (other than behaviourists) allow learning to be an interactive process, involving these internal events. These considerations tend to blur the distinction somewhat. Consequently, I would like to suggest the following working distinction: learning refers to actions, beliefs, and so on, that come about either through direct imitation of others, or as a conditioned response to punishments and rewards; invention refers to actions, beliefs, and so on, that result from internal processes of thinking and working out solutions to problems (though acknowledging that such processes are influenced by the individual's experience). The difference is in the degree to which internal, cognitive processes are seen as being involved in producing the response.

The most famous of criminology's learning theories, differential association, highlights some problems that result from this uneasy relationship between external and internal factors that have been used to distinguish learning from invention. Originated and developed by sociologists (Sutherland and Cressey, 1970) the theory was clearly intended to incorporate interactive and internal, cognitive processes. But because this left it so generalised as to sometimes appear to be saying hardly anything at all, it was open to imperialist take-over by more established, but much more mechanistic learning theories such as behaviourism.

Differential association starts with the observation that we all grow up in environments where we receive, from our associates, definitions both favourable and unfavourable to the acquisition of the motives for and the techniques to commit crime. The theory states that if we receive an excess of definitions favourable over those unfavourable, then we will commit crime. It allows that some definitions will be of greater 'priority and intensity' than others and this has been taken to imply that the definitions will differ in their subjective interpretation by those who receive them (see Taylor, Walton and Young, 1973). But this causes problems from the hard-line positivist point of view: if 'definitions' can vary in terms of such nebulous things as subjective meanings, how can they possibly be counted and measured? In a study attempting to utilise the theory, Cressey (1953) concluded that they probably could not be.

Cressey (1962) himself saw that the lack of specificity on the actual process of learning was a problem with the theory, but pointed out that Sutherland had left it open to clarification in the light of future developments in learning theory. Perhaps inevitably, this left it open to attempted incorporation by behaviourist psychology: Burgess and Akers (1966) provided a translation of differential association into the language of behaviourist 'reinforcement' theory. All this achieved was to take on the even more serious problems of behaviourism itself.[2] Taylor, Walton and Young (1973) were highly critical of this example of behaviourist imperialism and claimed that the exclusion of all reference to subjective mental events which the take-over bid necessarily entailed was entirely alien to the whole spirit of differential association. Although this is true in relation to the intellectual background from which both Sutherland and Cressey were writing, it is nevertheless the case that Cressey, in particular, was sufficiently part of the positivist tradition to be interested in a precise, quantifiable theory which did not automatically rule out such mechanistic approaches. The commitment to a *learning theory* which explained all crime clearly required the specification of empirically identifiable learning processes if it was to progress beyond the simple assertion that crime is learned.

In practice, it is difficult to see how learning theories could explain crime without any reference to invention. If crime is learned from others (as differential association proposes) where did it come from in the first place? Presumably, in the distant past, somebody must have invented it (in the sense that I have defined invention earlier). But if someone in the past was capable of inventing it, why cannot other people be inventing it now? In other words, to solve the 'origins' problem of learning theories it is necessary to propose an invention theory which then becomes an equally plausible explanation of *all* crime. To take a specific example, Lemert's (1958) study of cheque forgers found that they had not, typically, associated with other cheque forgers or people favourably disposed towards it; cheque forgery had not been handed down from some primeval inventor. The inescapable conclusion was that people were continually managing to think it up for themselves.

The idea that we are influenced by our environment, especially our social environment (family, friends and associates) seems unexceptionable. The problems seem to arise when this relationship is couched in terms of a 'learning theory'. The more literally this is interpreted the more it seems to lead into mechanistic, one-way formulations such as behaviourism. The more open it is to cognitive, interactive and voluntaristic elements, the more misleading seems the whole vocabulary of learning theory as a means of describing it. Differential association is a good illustration of these two contradictory tendencies. The positivist learning theory side of it did, despite protestations to the contrary, make possible the intrusion of the likes of Burgess and Akers. Its voluntaristic side, influenced as it was by the ideas of G. H. Mead, had more affinity with the analyses of the acquisition of motives, techniques, and so on, that were to characterise the 'symbolic interactionist revolution' of the 1960s. However, as we shall see, this revolution represented not only a movement away from the strict tenets of learning theory, but away from the assumptions and concerns of positivist criminology itself.

Invention

Some learning theories (differential association was an example) moved away from the idea of criminals being identifiably different kinds of people: their criminal behaviour was seen as being acquired in much the same way as any other behaviour was acquired; it did not require any special, predisposing characteristics for it to happen to particular people. On this view, criminals are still 'differentiated' – but only in terms of values, motives and skills favourable to the commission of crime, and these could be acquired by anyone given the right circumstances. This view characterises most sociological explanations of crime, including those that fall into the third category of causal explanation: invention.

In the previous subsection I distinguished invention from learning by stressing the extent to which the former involves internal processes of thinking and working out solutions to problems. In this sense invention seems to imply that crime is the outcome of the kind of rational decision-making that is associated with the classical criminological view (and I will suggest later that it is much the same idea). But sociological explanations of this kind have nevertheless been incorporated into the general category of positivist criminology because of their implication that the invention is not freely made but *forced*: some problem confronted by individuals in their environment *pushes* them out of convention and into crime. As in the case of learning theories, it is the *compelling*, *determining* influence of the individual's environmental experience that provides the link with positivism (though in the case of invention some room is still left for internal, cognitive processes in arriving at the solution).

By far the most important problem that has been selected as providing the push into the invention of crime has been *thwarted conventional ambitions* – Merton's (1938) 'anomie' theory and the 'delinquent subculture' theories of Cohen (1955) and Cloward and Ohlin (1960) being the most influential examples. In anomie theory the impetus that pushes people into crime is that the ambitions for status and pecuniary success that they share with everyone else are thwarted by the restrictions on the opportunities to achieve them that result from low socio-economic status. They are consequently forced into cheating. Delinquent subculture theory locates the impetus more specifically in the social setting of lower-class adolescent males (who were shown to be the most crime-prone by official statistics): they are disadvantaged in their quest for status and achievement (defined by conventional agencies such as the school) and consequently construct their own, alternative criteria. They use delinquent criteria in order to distance themselves as far as possible from conventional ones, and hence insulate themselves from a sense of failure. In all cases the lower-class 'victims' are pushed from a natural state of conformity into a state of delinquency by the relative lack of availability of conventional means to achieve conventional goals. Delinquent subculture theory, with its emphasis on a *collective* solution to the problem, also allowed for social learning to augment and expedite the generation of delinquent values.

The basic themes established by these four writers stimulated a truly enormous literature which dominated sociological thinking about crime in the 1950s and 1960s. Again, it is not my intention here to review the variations and criticisms in detail – this has been done many times elsewhere.[3] Rather, I would like to consider some of the more fundamental problems that are connected with the general nature of 'sociological positivism' and its relation to classical criminology.

One problem of these theories was, strangely enough, the obverse of the problem with the biological and personality-type theories. The latter, it may be re-membered, tended to generate categories (for example, biological or personality types) that could only possibly incorporate small amounts of criminal behaviour; that is, they explained *too little* crime. The sociological theories, on the other hand worked with categories that explained *too much* crime (what Matza, 1964, called the 'embarrassment of riches' problem). This is because they relied on features common to the whole of the lower class (restricted legitimate opportunities); these were very common, crime relatively rare. Even the weaker version – that the theories simply implied a *relationship* between low social class and crime – came later to be dismissed as an artefact of class-biased law enforcement (however, the argument about the relationship between social class and crime is a complex one to which I shall be returning in Part Two). Actually, the 'embarrassment of riches' problem boils down to the *same* failing as that of the biological and personality-type theories: they both produced categories that were, apparently, far too weakly related to crime to be worthy of a 'positivist' discipline.

It seems perfectly reasonable to assume that people who frequently commit crime hold 'pro-criminal' values. For delinquent subculture theories this assumption was vital; the term itself defines a different ('sub')culture from the host culture, the difference being that the 'subcultural' values are 'delinquent'. Perhaps because it seems so obvious, the theorists did not bother to try to find out whether delinquents did in fact hold delinquent values, but concentrated more on explaining how these values came about. When Matza (1964) did enquire into the matter (using his attack on subcultural theory as a basis for attacking positivist criminology generally) he found it simply was not the case: on the whole delinquents seemed to hold very conventional values. Oddly enough, given that this was part of an attack on positivism generally, Matza used the traditional tool of positivism (the questionnaire) to make the point. However, he did not use it very well – not bothering with a control group, for example (perhaps this was his concession to anti-positivism). Later, more rigorous studies (Hirschi, 1969; Hindelang, 1974) complicated the picture; delinquents were predominantly conventional in their values, but were less so than non-delinquents. But the problem was still there; even in relation to this seemingly most obvious of variables, the differentiation of criminals from non-criminals, which was so important to positivist criminology, failed to stand out adequately.

The theme of thwarted conventional ambitions that was essential to both anomie and delinquent subculture theories implied that criminals and delinquents suffered from a 'gap' between their aspirations and expectations, and the existence of such a gap came to be taken as the measure of the validity of the theories. Unfortunately it almost invariably failed to materialise; delinquents seemed to be, if anything, even more 'realistic' in their aspirations than non-delinquents (see, for example, Hirschi, 1969). Part of this problem seemed to stem from the fundamental assumption of such theories that everyone is, initially at least, conventional (the opposite of the assumption of classical criminology). This required some disturbance ('strain' as Hirschi calls it) – such as the 'gap' – to push them out of convention and into crime. It was the reversal of the classical position that was causing the problem. Yet in other respects, as was mentioned earlier, anomie-based 'invention' theories seemed to have much in common with classical criminology in their assumptions about human behaviour. In Part Two I will suggest that if they are pushed a little closer to the classical position, via some judicious reinterpretation, the problems dealt with above are eased considerably.

Positivism and Penal Treatment

One of the features by which positivism was characterised earlier was its inclusion of the idea of 'pathology': not only was crime seen as obviously wrong, but there was also something wrong with the people who did it – for example, in their biology or personality. In the sociological theories the pathology was to some extent transferred from the make-up of individual criminals to their social settings, although there was still an individual manifestation of that pathology in their pro-criminal values. For positivist criminology, as with its classical predecessor, crime was clearly a problem that begged a solution. The shift of focus from the crime to the criminal, however, seemed to be accompanied by a diversion of attention away from specific considerations of appropriate penal treatments. For most positivist criminologists such concerns were often left to an appendix to their main causal concerns, or omitted altogether. This was partly because it was felt that a true understanding of the causes of crime was necessary *before* a clear corrective programme could be enunciated and that point, of course, was never quite reached – 'more research' was always needed. Also, deriving cures from causes is not as straightforward as it might seem: sometimes the causes are factors that are not very readily manipulable.

Although the original biological positivists' work was overwhelmingly concerned with the causes of crime, they *were* associated with a particular penal programme as well. Or rather, they laid down specific principles that were to be more or less taken for granted by subsequent positivists. Penal practice was another area that they wanted to make 'scientific'. As we have already seen, this involved the abandonment of the metaphysics of freedom, responsibility and desert in favour of the practical objectives of reformation, prevention and the protection of society. Their specific programme was derived from their conception of the causes of crime. In their later writings they had been forced to acknowledge, in the light of much critical evidence, that their biologically determined criminal was only one of a variety of types: their theory had become eclectic and multi-factorial. Consequently, a variety of reformative treatments were necessary to suit the different requirements of different types of offender. Treatment was to be *individualised*, based on scientific assessment and classification. Ferri (1967, p. 443) proposed three principles:

(a) An equilibrium of right and protection must be established between the individual to be judged and the society which judges in order to escape the exaggerations . . . introduced by the classical school, which failed to distinguish between dangerous and not dangerous, atavistic and evolutive delinquents.

(b) The duty of a criminal judge is not to determine the degree of moral responsibility of a delinquent but his material guilt or physical responsibility, and this once proven, to fix the form of social preservation best suited to the defendant according to the anthropological category to which he belongs.

(c) Continuity and solidarity between the different practical divisions of social defence from the judiciary police to sentence and execution.

The first principle reiterates a point made earlier: although they favoured reform rather than punishment, this was not for humanitarian reasons. They saw the mixture of deterrence and retribution that characterised neoclassical criminology as too soft – favouring criminals' rights at the expense of the protection of society. Garland (1985a) notes three themes in their programme: reform, prevention – and *extinction*; those who could not be reformed were to be eliminated.

The biological positivists did not, however, involve themselves in the detailed specification of penal treatments. And subsequently, the practical discipline of 'penology' tended to become separated from 'criminology proper'. To some extent this reflected the accepted division between 'science' and 'policy-making' as intellectual activities; policy-making involved value judgements, and these were simply not appropriate to the 'objective' scientist. This was particularly the case with sociological theories where such judgements were, inevitably, politically loaded.

Wilson (1975) has suggested another reason for the division between positivist criminology and penology: the causal variables that were proposed related to areas that were difficult to change – especially with the limited powers and resources available to penal practitioners. Genetic make-up, early childhood socialisation, class divisions and inequalities of opportunity are things which we either do not know how to change, or would involve a degree of social and economic transformation which is very unlikely to be embarked on in the name of reducing crime.

Good examples of intractable causal variables are those that relate to genetic make-up. The biological positivists could only propose indeterminate detention or extinction for such categories of offender. Their forced accommodation to the existence of a wide range of non-genetic categories saved them from being solely associated with such a negative approach. However, since these latter categories were derived from lay 'common-sense' beliefs rather than the scientific rigour they advocated so much (see Wolfgang, 1960; and Garland, 1985a), their specific reformative recommendations tended not to amount to very much either. Interestingly, Eysenck (1977) seems to encounter the same kind of problem. At the end of a book almost entirely devoted to arguing for a strong genetic component in the causes of crime, he turns his attention to the contemporary 'crime wave' and what should be done about it. He concludes that changes in genetic factors obviously cannot explain the crime wave. Rather, it can only be explained in terms of a massive decline in the quality of conditioning of children: 'We live in an era of permissiveness and thus have largely abandoned all attempts to inculcate standards, values and "conscience" into our children' (ibid., p. 209). The cure is a return to the traditional values of discipline in the home, school, and so on. Like the biological positivists before him, after a long treatise devoted to 'scientific rigour' he suddenly turns, at the crucial point, to unrigorous lay belief.

Generally speaking, however, those psychological theories that have located the cause of crime in problems in early childhood 'socialisation' have tended to have closer links with both penological thinking and practice. They also tend to be associated with more specific therapeutic practices, derived from the tenets of the particular psychological theory; for example, psychoanalytic theories are associated with various forms of psychotherapy, and behaviourist-type theories are associated with different versions of conditioning. And the more general view that the causes of crime are located in problems in early family relationships has, of course, been incorporated into most criminal jurisdictions.

The relationship between sociological theories of the causes of crime and theories about its treatment is much more tenuous. Because these theories stressed social structural features such as inequality of opportunity, proposing cures involved entering into political debate, endangering the theorists' stance as objective scientists 'just giving the facts'. They consequently tended to be rather coy about drawing corrective conclusions from their theories. Merton (1938), for example, does not conclude his exposition of anomie theory by proposing a solution (though he gives enough away elsewhere for Taylor, Walton and Young, 1973, to see him as favouring a 'meritocratic' solution). Cohen (1955) devotes only three pages to the control of delinquent subcultures and states that 'from a diagnosis of a social ill, even a correct one, the "right" solution does not leap to the eye in any obvious way' (ibid., p. 177). The rest of his discussion in these few pages is about how all sorts of possible answers *could* be proposed, involving the 'balancing of social values'. Cloward and Ohlin (1960), in a highly influential work did not themselves draw any treatment conclusions (although their ideas inspired a major treatment programme). The key textbooks of sociological theories did sometimes conclude with a discussion of treatment implications, but often in the form of an analysis of existing provisions with occasional nods of approval or disapproval. A good example would be the many editions of Sutherland and Cressey (1970). In the course of their analysis they state the following:

> Thus crime would be prevented by modifying those who can be modified, segregating those who cannot be so modified, correcting in advance of crime those who are proved to be most likely to commit crime, and attacking and eliminating the social situations which are most conducive to crime (ibid., p. 608).

The most striking feature of this is its similarity to the 'reform, prevention and extinction' ascribed to Ferri earlier (except that the 'extinction' is replaced by the more moderate 'segregation'). However, Sutherland and Cressey do go on to include a consideration of poverty, unemployment, bad housing, and the like, under the heading of 'social situations which are most conducive to crime'. But, perhaps sensing dangerous moral and political overtones, they add (ibid., p. 634, quoting Taft): 'It is not the task of the criminologist to determine what is the major social good'.

It would be misleading to suggest that there was anything approaching a complete intellectual segregation between criminology and penology, even in their sociological versions. And where the two overlapped it is possible to discern a general acceptance of the basic positivist principles of individualised rehabilitation, prevention and societal protection. But there was a general reluctance on the part of positivist criminologists, especially the later ones, to draw clear-cut corrective conclusions from their causal analyses.

In the case of the sociological positivists, this reluctance applied even when they *did* become involved in the analysis of the operation of penal institutions – when the 'sociology of the prison blossomed in the 1950s and 1960s. In 1958 Clemmer's *The Prison Community* was reissued and, in the same year, Sykes's *The Society of Captives* was published. These two books initiated a substantial body of sociological research into the 'social world' of the prison.[4] The focus was on the social relationships in the prison (especially the informal ones), prison culture, argot roles and the 'inmate code'. Despite this direct involvement with the penal process, the spirit was decidedly anti-correctionalist: the intention was to provide an appreciative understanding of the prison social world. Sometimes the findings were examined for their implications for the effectiveness of prisons in preventing recidivism (European Committee on Crime Problems, 1967), but this was a side issue: the sociology of the prison was not about devising effective treatment programmes. Anyway, the news was not good: the findings emphasised a resilient, informal inmate code based on anti-prison, anti-therapeutic values acting as a bulwark against the 'pains' and indignities of imprisonment. If anything, these studies had more in common with the avowedly anti-correctionalist 'labelling' theories of the later 1960s.

The basic principles of penal treatment that I have portrayed as running through most positivist criminological theorising, also became incorporated into penal practice. In Britain, this began to happen at about the same time as the emergence of positivist criminology – though, again, this is not to suggest any simple causal relation, in either direction (see Garland, 1985b). Nor must this process be exaggerated: as Bottoms (1983) has pointed out, by far the most significant development in penal practice this century, in sheer quantitative terms, has been the increased use of the fine – and this expresses classical 'deterrence-through-symbolism' rather than positivist principles. Nevertheless, the twentieth century also witnessed a significant movement towards the acceptance of the principles of assessment, diversity of provision, rehabilitation, segregation and prevention, into penal practice. This had the effect of making the penal system available as a 'laboratory' for testing positivist principles of correction, as well as for providing the bodies for testing their causal theories. The positivist commitment to the achievement of empirical goals such as causally relevant variables and effective penal treatments (rather than such nebulous things as 'justice' and 'desert') required it to be subjected to such empirical assessment. This proved to be one of the sources of its downfall: there came a point when failure to come up with the goods, rationalised by 'the need for more research', began to sound a little hollow and begged the asking of more fundamental questions. And this was what happened in the 1960s and 1970s – the subject of the next chapter.

Positivism and Classicism

At the beginning of this chapter it was suggested that the main features by which we can characterise the wider category of positivist criminology (and which also serve to distinguish it from classical criminology) are determinism, differentiation, pathology and the diversion of attention away from crime (and the criminal law) to the criminal. To conclude, it would be useful to reconsider these categories in the light of the preceding discussion.

Determinism and differentiation are inextricably linked in the positivist programme: the determinants are identified by the way they make criminals differ from non-criminals. Positivist causal theories stand or fall by the extent to which they are able to establish the existence of 'types' of human beings (whether in terms of biology, personality, or values) who are crime-prone. As we have seen, they had tended to fall – no such clear-cut categories seem to have emerged. The best that we seem to be able to say is that biological and psychological categories have tended to contain only a very small minority of offenders (as well as a significant proportion of non-offenders), while sociological categories have contained a large majority of non-offenders (and by no means all offenders).

Perhaps part of the problem is that far too much has been expected of positivist criminology or, alternatively, positivist criminologists have been responsible for fostering too grandiose expectations. In its most basic sense, determinism is only committed to the view that behaviour is the outcome of antecedent causes. It allows for a multiplicity of different causes acting in different combinations on different people in different situations (it even allows that every particular criminal act may result from a *unique* constellation of antecedent causes). On this view, we can only realistically expect positivist criminology to produce 'probabilistic' theories – associating variability of cause with variability of outcome; we should expect no more than loose associations between specified causal variables and criminal behaviour.

An interesting consequence of taking this much looser view of determinism is that it brings us much closer to the classical position. Classical criminology clearly allows for a loose association between antecedent variables and outcomes: the probability of crime varies according to the degree of rationality of individuals and the efficiency and consistency of the criminal justice system. The difference between this and the more probabilistic version of determinism is in what it is that is seen as being responsible for the 'looseness' of the association. In classical criminology it is our ability to make free choices and resist so-called causal pressures; in the determinist version it is the fact that there is an unknowable amount of other causal variables in play, pulling in varying directions. But, as Hook has pointed out (see Matza, 1964, pp. 10–11), *in practice* the two positions are virtually identical: both 'free choice' and 'unknown causes' manifest themselves in *unpredictability*. The 'free' person and the person who acts from an unknowable constellation of causes are difficult to distinguish; the problem of explaining their behaviour is, for all practical purposes, the same. To the extent that positivist criminology incorporates a realistic, manageable version of determinism, it becomes compatible with its classical predecessor.

An example of the practical similarity between determinist and indeterminist positions occurred earlier in the difficulty that was encountered in identifying sociological 'invention' theories, such as anomie, as being in the deterministic, positivist tradition (where writers such as Jeffery and Matza have located them). 'Pure' invention is akin to 'pure' free choice. Yet as was noted, inventions, like choices, are always constrained by social experiential factors such as available opportunities and knowledge of alternatives; even the most ardent indeterminist would acknowledge such things (while still holding out for an irreducible residue of free choice). But this seems also to be the stance of anomie theory: the anomic individuals are clearly pushed and constrained yet, within those constraints, they manage to invent rational solutions (in the sense that these solutions come about through internal reasoning processes, rather than as an autonomic response). Admittedly, anomie theory accentuates the constraints rather more than would perhaps be acceptable to indeterminists, but this is simply a matter of emphasis rather than qualitative difference from a 'realistic' indeterminist position.

The important difference between sociological invention theorists and classicists is not so much in their ultimate stances on determinism, but in their assumptions about the nature and consequences of human motives, and in the degree to which they saw criminals as being differentiated from non-criminals. Anomie theorists and their subcultural followers reversed the classical position on these matters, and in doing so encountered serious problems. They assumed that we are all naturally motivated towards convention and require some force ('strain') to push us out of it. In turn, this implied that deviants should exhibit a 'gap' between their conventional aspirations and expectations, and should be clearly differentiated from non-deviants by their adherence to oppositional values (neither of which turned out to be the case).

As we have seen, classicism allows for a much more complex human relationship with deviance and conformity, with a natural, self-interested potentiality for both. Using this as a starting point, we would not expect the kinds of social pressure defined by anomie-type theories to force change from one finite state to the other. Rather, we would simply expect the relative *demotion* of conformity (in terms of both goals and means) as against deviance, because it offers less. There would be no reason to expect either the 'gap' or the clear commitment to deviant values that have been such persistent stumbling blocks for the traditional versions of these theories.

In Part Two I will suggest a way in which the important contribution that anomie theory makes to understanding crime can be reformulated in classical terms, much to its benefit.

The third defining feature of positivist criminology – pathology – is closely related to differentiation. In fact, as we have seen, it boils down to a moral evaluation of differentiation (rather than a 'scientific' finding): the differences that distinguish criminals are things that are deemed to have 'gone wrong' with their biology, psyche or values. As such, of course, it fails to the extent that the attempt to establish the differentiation fails. If criminals on the whole are not clearly differentiated from non-criminals, it is difficult to explain their crime in terms of something having gone wrong with them (except in the tautological sense that the commission of the crime itself represents something having gone wrong with them).

As in the case of classical criminology, positivist criminology embodied an assumption that there is some objective category of 'crime' that is obviously wrong and needs something doing about it. Classical criminology did not assume that existing legal definitions of crime and the way they are enforced necessarily constitute this objective category. Similarly, as we saw, positivists tended to recognise the need for a category of 'crime' outside of the existing legal one. But *in practice* positivists almost invariably worked uncritically and unquestioningly with the products of the existing legal definitions; *by default*, they endowed them with an objective status. This, of course, stemmed from their general lack of interest in the significance of the criminal justice system – the final feature that distinguishes them from classical criminology.

The division seems almost complete: classical criminology focused entirely on the causal-corrective significance of the criminal justice system and ignored individual, social and economic factors; positivist criminology focused almost entirely on the causal significance of individual, social and economic factors and ignored the criminal justice system. The latter is not entirely true, of course: the sociologists of the prison did provide evidence of causal significance in the effects of imprisonment, as we saw (even if it was not, usually, their concern to do so). In neither case was the omission a necessary consequence of the intellectual stance of the two schools. We saw in Chapter 1 that there was no logical reason for classical criminology's omission of individual, social and economic factors. Positivist criminologists' omission of the causal significance of the operations of the criminal justice system is perhaps even more of an oddity: they sought causes of crime in the social world of the criminal, and yet omitted legal processes as being a significant part of that social world!

Although positivist criminologists ignored the *causal* implications of the criminal justice system, they were fairly uniformly associated with a specific *corrective programme*, even though this was not their primary concern. As was pointed out at the beginning of this chapter, they shared classical criminology's view that the purpose of penal practice was effective crime control. But their view on how this should be achieved was quite different: correction was to be an applied science whose goal, where feasible, was to be the rehabilitation of individual offenders (where it was not feasible, segregation or elimination, for the protection of society, was to suffice). But they tended not to become involved outside of their support for these very general principles. As we saw, this was partly because their stance of 'scientific detachment' precluded too close an involvement in matters of 'policy' and partly because the causes of crime that they generated tended to involve factors that were beyond the scope of penal practitioners. For these reasons they tended to be much less closely associated with the advocacy of specific legal and penal reforms than classical criminology was.

In Chapter 1 it was suggested that Beccaria may have felt inhibited in including economic and social conditions in his programme because of their dangerous political implications. The positivists seem to have tried to avoid this problem by, once again, adopting the 'scientific' stance. When they considered social and economic factors they saw themselves as detached scientists just 'presenting the facts' and not (as Taft (1942, p. 634) put it) aiming 'to determine what is the major social good'. So although positivist criminology did concern itself with social and economic conditions, in a way that classical criminology did not, it mostly ended up just as timid-looking as far as drawing 'corrective' conclusions was concerned.

It is tempting to conclude that perhaps there could be a complementary relationship between positivist and classical criminology – one providing the focus on individual, social and economic factors, the other on penal and legal ones. This seems particularly the case if we draw them closer together in their positions on determinism, along the lines suggested earlier. But before this could be contemplated, there are some more serious problems with the positivist stance that would have to be resolved – again relating to its neglect of criminal justice processes. For it was the complex machinations of these processes that provided the 'data' on crime and criminals that positivist criminologists used to build their theories. Their assumption that this could be ignored, and the data assumed to be objective representations of crime and criminality, was to prove to be one of their greatest weaknesses, as we shall see in the next chapter.

Notes

1 A reasonable cross-section of books assessing the range of positivist criminology would be provided by the following: Taylor, Walton and Young (1973); Downes and Rock (1982); Hall Williams (1982); Rutter and Giller (1983).
2 Still probably the best (and wittiest) critique of behaviourism is provided by Koestler (1970, Chapter 1). In relation to behaviourist criminology see Taylor, (1971, Chapter 4); and Halbasch (1979).
3 See Clinard (1964); Yablonsky (1962); Short and Strodtbeck (1965); Downes (1966); Patrick (1973) and Matza (1964).
4 In addition to Clemmer (1958) and Sykes (1958), see Cressey (1961); Cloward *et al.* (1960); European Committee on Crime Problems (1967); Mathieson (1965); Giallombardo (1966; 1974).

3 Reassessment: Classical and Anti-classical Themes in the 1960s and 1970s

Classical criminology reflected contemporary ideas about the social contract, rationality and utility; positivist criminology celebrated what seemed to be the successful application of science and technology to human beings. Behind both we may, if we wish (and many do), suggest causal relationships between such ideas and changing social and economic conditions and the supposed needs of dominant social classes. My concern, however, has been the more modest one of simply characterising and comparing classical and positivist ideas. Where such ideas ultimately came from and what practical consequences they have had are questions which, on the whole, I have preferred to avoid.

However, we can directly relate the intellectual ideas of the 1960s about crime and criminals with events in the world, because the proponents themselves acknowledged the connection. Things happened in this period that profoundly influenced sociological thinking in particular, and especially in so far as it related to crime and criminals; they led to a comprehensive rejection of the most cherished principles of positivist criminology. Incorporated in this revolt was both the resurrection of classical principles and the development of new ones that appear to be incompatible. Both sets of principles will be the subject of this chapter. But first, a little more on the background to their emergence.

The 1960s and early 1970s have been characterised by Pearson (1975), perhaps rather extravagantly, as the period of 'the great refusal'. The central focus of that 'refusal' was the opposition to the involvement of the United States in the Vietnam War. Loosely linked to it were the emerging environmentalist movements (the link being forged by a deep suspicion of advanced technology which had raised the spectre of nuclear holocaust and then manifested itself in the devastation inflicted on Vietnam). An additional kind of refusal was provided by the activities of the various civil rights movements, starting with blacks, then incorporating gay and women's liberation. Caught up in these movements was the hippie culture of the period, with its involvement with hallucinogenic drugs. What these various movements had in common was that they provoked confrontations, first in the United States and then to a lesser extent in Britain, which highlighted features of law and its enforcement that made academic, positivist criminology look extremely complacent and conservative.

It became particularly apparent that 'crimes' were not absolutes that could be taken for granted as being 'obviously wrong' in the way that positivist criminology seemed to do. Rather they appeared as a selection – and a selection that seemed to reflect the interests of the powerful. Thus, much was made of the fact that while the war in Vietnam was 'legal', protesting against it was liable to lead to the protester being defined as a criminal; that drinking alcohol was respectable, while smoking cannabis was not. Such observations highlighted the fact that 'criminal' was a status that was conferred upon particular acts, reflecting particular power interests. Yet positivist criminology had, as we have seen, almost completely ignored such processes, concerning itself solely with criminals and the causes of their criminality. Perhaps not surprisingly, the 'new' criminologists insisted that attention should be redirected to the *definers* of crime. In doing so, they extended the field of interest to *all* those acts which are adversely defined and stigmatised – that is, from *crime* to the wider category of *deviance*.

For similar reasons, the new sociologists of deviance were hostile to what appeared to them to be the reduction of crime to a 'technical' problem. Positivist criminology seemed to represent another example of the misuse of technology – in this case in its application to human beings themselves. Crime had been portrayed by positivists as a pathology, requiring the application of psychological or sociological technology to put it right; criminals were seen as a kind of societal waste product requiring hygienic processing. When 'criminals' were seen to include protesters against war, pollution and the infringement of minority rights, or people who preferred cannabis to alcohol, such a view was seen as highly offensive. It was here, too, that broader links were formed with other kinds of social deviance which had similarly been reduced to technical problems. Thus, 'mental illness' was seen as a label by which genuine human responses to oppressive social conditions were reduced to mental faults, requiring technical (in this case medical) solutions; for a while the 'new deviance' attempted to incorporate writers as different as R. D. Laing and Thomas Szasz from what was temporarily known as 'anti-psychiatry'.

The rejection of the pathological view of crime required a concomitant rejection of the 'correctionalist' stance of positivist criminology. The new deviance writers were naturally anxious to disengage themselves from association with such conservative goals. A favoured alternative was Matza's (1969) 'appreciative' stance; the aim of the new sociologist of deviance was to enter into and appreciate the meaning world of the deviant. The new view also required a rejection of the basic determinism of positivist criminology. It favoured a more voluntaristic conception of human action – a need to see human beings fighting back against an oppressive state, and capable of making things happen. Indeed, Matza's appreciation of the deviant sometimes extended, in other writers, to endowing the deviant with an embryonic revolutionary or even transcendental consciouness. Against this, positivist criminology's deterministic conception was hopelessly stifling and fatalistic.

It was this interplay of ideas and practical events that lay behind the 'interactionist revolution' of the 1960s and 1970s and was to have a powerful influence over both psychological and sociological thinking about crime and deviance. As this brief background has perhaps already suggested, it incorporated themes with a distinctly classical flavour to them; sometimes, as we will see, this connection was acknowledged. In other respects, however, it seems quite different. The picture is further complicated by the appearance, at roughly the same time, of classical themes from sources that, in other respects, were much closer to positivist criminology. This chapter is an attempt to sort these various pro- and anti-classical elements in to some kind of order.

Classical Themes in the 'New Sociology of Deviance'

It seemed that the circumstances of the 1960s favoured, for the more radical and involved academic, a relativistic conception of crime and a more positive, voluntaristic conception of the criminal or deviant. The new 'sociologists of deviance' who emerged from this background have been loosely grouped under the headings of *symbolic interactionists, transactionalists* and *societal reaction* theorists. They can be broadly characterised by the work of Matza (1964; 1969), Becker (1963; 1964), Lemert (1967) and Goffman (1968a; 1968b) in the United States, and Cohen (1971), Taylor and Taylor (1973) and Phillipson (1971) in Britain, among many others.

The *interactionist perspective* (as it is most familiarly known) proved in the end to be unable to incorporate all the radical demands that came to be made of it. But, initially at least, it seemed to express the right kinds of sentiment. It was based in part on the resurrection of ideas originally propounded by G. H. Mead. Human beings are seen as constructing their actions in a process of interaction with others via the use of symbols, such as language – hence 'symbolic interactionism'. But we are not seen merely as passive recipients in these interaction processes; we bring our own autonomous motives and meanings to bear on them – we are at least partially 'free'. An important feature of these interactions, which was to play a major part in the new interactionism, was that we use stereotypical 'labels' to make sense of other people, based on cues or knowledge that we have about them. One such important label is that of *criminal* (or *deviant*). The main thesis of the interactionists was that the 'official' application of these particular labels (via agencies such as school-teachers and police) had profound consequences for the persons so labelled, and for the way we perceive and understand crime and deviance. In other words, to explain or understand crime and deviance we must be at least as much concerned with the activities of the *conferers* of these labels as with the *recipients*.

Matza (1964) explicitly portrayed these kinds of idea as involving a partial return to classicism. As we saw in Chapter 2, in his criticism of subcultural theory Matza favoured a return to the less deterministic, less differentiated view of the criminal that was characteristic of classical criminology – though, in his later work (Matza, 1969) he moved to a more fully indeterminist view. In the earlier book he had proposed an additional reversion to classical principles: that the focus of attention be switched back from the criminal to the crime. This involved, as with classical criminology, a consideration of the significance of the operations of the criminal justice system – a similar focus to that of the more general interactionist concern with the conferers of criminal and deviant labels. Matza thus highlighted the link between the assumptions and concerns of classical criminology with those of the new interactionists. His own contribution was to suggest ways in which the legal process exerted a powerful influence over delinquents: it provided them with a vocabulary which enabled them to justify their delinquent actions 'in the circumstances' ('techniques of neutralisation') and with a sense of injustice which helped to release them from feelings of obligation to conform. As this suggests, although his focus was the same as that of classical criminology, the conclusions that Matza came to about the influence of the criminal justice system seem to be rather different. When we consider the more general conclusions that emerged from the other interactionists' concern with 'the labellers', the divergence becomes even more apparent.

For example, interactionists took a much more profoundly relativistic view of crime than the original classical position allowed for. They emphasised that crimes are defined by processes of human deliberation and that those definitions are then applied by human agencies. To behave as if such human processes produce some kind of universal, objective category that can be taken for granted by criminologists was, they argued, absurd. 'Crimes' varied from place to place and from time-period to time-period; they reflected the interests, moral concerns and ideological positions of those who were in the power positions that defined and enforced them. To take existing definitions and enforcement practices for granted was in fact, they argued, to take a very specific – *conservative* – position. These arguments suggested that the starting point for criminology should be a consideration of how the legal rules that define crimes come about and whose interests they serve. And, indeed, they helped to establish a new resurgence of interest in the sociology of law.

Perhaps the most crucial point of these arguments from the point of view of positivist criminologists, however, was that these very human processes that define and enforce crimes produce the criminals and data on which positivists had built their theories. Criminal statistics are not produced by criminals – they are produced by people *defining* other people and acts as criminal. Admittedly, most positivists had acknowledged that there were problems with their data. However, after a statutory early chapter outlining these problems, the implications were invariably ignored in the serious empirical analysis and theorising that took place later. For the interactionists this was grossly inadequate. They emphasised that the data represented the successful application of labels to acts – on a highly selective basis, reflecting the kinds of people agents of control such as the police regard as likely suspects, or as being dangerous enough to warrant official action. The implications of such a view were potentially disastrous for positivist criminology. For example, the concentration of crime in the lower social class, which was the starting point for all the main sociological theories, could be explained simply by the fact that members of the lower social class were more likely to be selected for labelling. Similarly, if the police believed (thanks to psychological theories) that 'real' delinquents came from broken or otherwise disrupted homes, it could be that they would be more likely to take official action against offenders from such backgrounds, with the result that subsequent analysis of official 'delinquents' would automatically confirm the theories.

Since it is the public who report crime, and the police who decide whether to record such reports officially, crime *rates* and crime *trends* are also the products of the 'reactors to' rather than the 'doers of' crime. This meant that changes in crime rates, or variations between different settings (such as urban and rural), which had played an important part in theories relating social or economic conditions and change to crime, could equally well be explained by variations in crime-recording practices. Interactionists made much of how such variations could lead to a 'deviancy amplification spiral': if the public (informed by the media of rises in the criminal statistics) believes crime to be on the increase and more of a problem they may be more sensitive to it, report more to the police who will then record more and therefore produce a further rise in recorded crime, which is then fed back to the public by the media, and so on (see Wilkins, 1964; and Young, 1971).

Such arguments were not simply suggesting that criminal statistics were 'biased'. In Cicourel's (1968) analysis it seemed that the data presented a different kind of reality altogether: they *only* reflected the meanings, moral categories and stereotypes of those who collect and interpret the data; they told us nothing about criminals themselves (though in the Preface to the second edition Cicourel (1976) seemed to retreat from this more radical position). In the work of Bottomley and Coleman (1981) criminal statistics are so much a function of highly variable administrative practices that they seem almost incapable of telling us anything about anything.

The new deviance writers went further than suggesting that the *appearance* of crime (on which positivists built their theories) was in fact the product of the criminal justice system. The 'societal reaction' that defines crime and deviance was also seen as having a profound effect on the criminals and deviants themselves. Lemert (1967) proposed a second component to the 'amplification spiral' – what he called 'secondary deviance': a consequence of being officially labelled 'deviant' is that other people come to regard the labelled person differently, as a different *kind* of person. Lemert suggested that this cuts off access to conventional settings, activities and identities and in time leads to the 'deviants' acquiring a different conception of themselves: they live up to the deviant identity given to them by the labellers and indulge in *more* ('secondary') deviance.

Lemert's concept of secondary deviance perhaps represented the most thorough resurrection of the criminological concern with the criminal justice system. From counting for virtually nothing in positivist criminology it now seemed to count for everything, as it had originally done in classical criminology. Not only did it designate the nature and appearance of crime, but it also reappeared as *causally* implicated: in both classical criminology and the new deviance perspective, the amount of crime was primarily a function of the operations of the criminal justice system. But there was one rather important difference: in classical criminology the criminal justice system, properly reformed, was seen as the means of *reducing* crime. In the new perspective it seemed only capable of *increasing* it! Indeed, Schur (1973) was to develop the logic of this argument into a book entitled *Radical Non-intervention*.

However, it was in this reversal of the classical conclusion on the potentialities of the criminal justice system that interactionism encountered some of its more serious problems. One of these was a matter of internal consistency. As we have seen, one of the main intentions of interactionism was to get away from the conservative, causal-corrective stance that was seen as resulting from the determinism and absolutism of positivist criminology. While the idea that the response to crime actually caused more crime was pleasantly ironic, it was nevertheless still very much a causal-sounding theory, and one of a particularly deterministic nature. 'Labels' seemed to be highly constraining; once applied, the receivers seemed to have little say in what happened to them. The 'societal response' seemed to determine the outcome in much the same way, if not more so, as social and economic variables in sociological positivism. Indeed, it was the *same* social and economic variables (low socio-economic status and powerlessness) that 'explained' crime (though in quite a different way – by increasing vulnerability to labelling rather than by increasing actual deviation).

Interactionist writers later denied that they ever intended such deterministic conclusions. But they illustrated the difficulty of purging language of all causal terminology. Looking back on it, Lemert (1974, p. 458) both acknowledges and, unwittingly, illustrates the problem:

> The societal reactions approach sought to show how deviance was shaped and stabilised by efforts to ameliorate it. In retrospect, the break with structural conceptions of deviance and the traditional concerns of sociology with causes was by no means complete.

Presumably, Lemert is using 'shaped and stabilised' to avoid some more overtly causal expression. But it is difficult to see what this could mean other than that some deviance, at least, would not have occurred had it not been for the societal response – that is, had been caused by it. Similarly, it is difficult to construe his distinction between primary and secondary deviance as meaning anything other than that secondary deviance is *caused by* societal reaction and its consequences for the deviant. Young (1971), for example, utilising the primary-to-secondary progression in his study of drug-takers in Notting Hill, London, provides what seems like a highly deterministic causal explanation of this process.

Perhaps as a result of the unintended involvement in causal explanation the boundaries of, and empirical support for, 'labelling theory' as a causal explanation were not systematically explored. The fact that the majority of people officially labelled as 'criminal' by the criminal justice system for the first time, never are again, seems to be a restriction on labelling theory's potential in this respect. Nor was any indication given as to under what circumstances the minority 'labelling' effect occurred. Consequently it did not really manage to achieve the level of plausibility of the more popularly accepted opposite view of classical criminology – that official processing *deters* further deviant acts. However, the issue of the relationship between classical deterrence and interactionist 'labelling' clearly needs further attention, and I will be returning to it in Chapter 8.

Classicism and 'Control Theory'

The 'new deviance' writers resurrected one major theme of classical criminology (the significance of the criminal justice system), though they modified it considerably in doing so. Other themes reappeared at approximately the same time, but from quite different sources. Most notable was the 'control theory' developed by Hirschi (1969) and utilised by many others including, in Britain, Box (1981). Although rooted in the positivist tradition (especially in the case of Hirschi), control theories also owe a clear and acknowledged debt to the classical tradition.

Kornhauser (1978) has pointed out that the main tenets of control theory are to be found in the ideas of the pioneers of sociological criminology – the sociologists of the Chicago school, working in the early decades of this century (Thrasher, 1927; Shaw, 1929). These theorists accounted for the high rates of crime found in the broken-down inner-city areas in terms of 'social disorganisation'. By this they meant that the economic disadvantage, conflict of cultures and high mobility of these areas resulted in a lack of opportunities for the satisfaction of conventional needs, and the relative absence, or weakness, of conventional controls. In their portrayal, delinquency is seen as a natural and rational choice for residents of these areas. Thrasher's delinquent gang members are not seen as frustrated conventionalists 'forced' into crime, but rather as normal kids, with normal needs, making the best available choices to satisfy those needs, just like everyone else. These assumptions of the naturalness of deviation in the light of its relative costs and benefits are, of course, highly reminiscent of the classical position.

It was Hirschi (1969), however, who developed ideas such as these into a 'control theory'. His starting point was dissatisfaction with most sociological theories of crime (especially anomie and subcultural theories) for reasons which are now familiar: their assumption that we naturally conform to conventionally defined goals and the means of achieving them, and that we consequently require some 'push' (or 'strain', as Hirschi calls it) to propel us into crime. Hirschi's control theory reverts to a more classical starting assumption: that human motives are naturally diverse, often self-seeking and hence likely to favour violation of whatever rules there are defining 'crimes'. For control theory the question that requires answering is 'what causes people to conform?'

However, control theory does not take our diverse, potentially deviant motives as being expressive of 'free will' in the way that classical criminology does. Rather, it treats them as 'given', in the sense that it is seen as neither plausible nor fruitful to attempt a causal explanation of them. But as I suggested in the last part of Chapter 2, this difference is not of any great practical significance: whether deviant motivations are taken as given because they express free will (classical theory) or because it is not deemed fruitful to attempt their explanation (control theory) does not, in itself, have any practical implications for the subsequent criminological enterprise.

Another similarity between control theory and classical criminology is in the kinds of answer they give to the question 'why do we conform?'. In both cases the answer is that we will conform when we see it as being in our interests to do so. If it is not, then we will not. Control theory echoes the classical, utilitarian, 'rational self-seeking' view of human beings. However, the similarity ends there – there is no return to the vague, semi-mystical idea of a 'social contract'. Hirschi treats the question of what 'bonds' individuals to conformity as an empirical problem. He proposes four bonds: attachment (the extent to which individuals have close emotional ties to other people); commitment (the extent to which they see conventional behaviour, for example at school, as offering immediate or long-term rewards); involvement (the extent to which their time is taken up with conventional activities); belief (the extent to which their beliefs about what is permissible or not coincide with conventional ones). He subjects these bonds to rigorous empirical testing using the standard techniques of positivist criminology (survey, statistical analysis), while in addition attempting to avoid the problem of the selectivity of 'official' definitions of criminality by using alternative sources of data ('self-report' data).

Hirschi's control theory seems also to fill an important gap that was noted earlier in relation to the original formulation of classical criminology. Beccaria, it may be remembered, was criticised for only considering the disincentives associated with the operations of the criminal justice system in controlling crime, when the logic of his position clearly suggested the relevance of *all* incentives and disincentives for conformity or deviance encountered by individuals in their social settings. Control theory partly rectifies this: Hirschi focuses almost exclusively on the incentives for conformity that are built in (or not) to individuals' relationships with, and expectations of, their more immediate social environment, such as parents, peers, school and local community. However, Hirschi does not consider the wider social context in which these relationships operate, in the way that earlier sociological theories did. This is because he rejects social class differences and class-based theories such as anomie as explanations of crime – partly because of their 'strain' assumption, and partly because his data (which use sources other than 'official' ones) fail to support the existence of a class differential. Also, his different bonds to conformity are not fully independent of each other, with a tendency towards being reducible to the primary bond of attachment – particularly to parents. This tends further to narrow the social context of his variables.

Nevertheless, Hirschi considerably extends the focus of the original classical formulation beyond the criminal justice system, and towards considering incentives towards conformity rather than disincentives towards deviation. Indeed, he reverses the classical emphasis since he gives no consideration at all to the significance of the criminal justice system in controlling crime. In Hirschi's version of control theory people conform because they perceive benefits in doing so, and fear losing them. When they do not perceive any such benefits, they feel free to deviate. It is the failure of incentives, not the failure of disincentives, that is crucial. In this respect Hirschi shared the long-standing positivist rejection of the central tenet of classicism: deterrence. As Gibbs (1975, p. 11) points out, in a book marking a later resurgence of interest, the positivist eclipse of classicism led to an almost total loss of interest in deterrence in the writings of criminologists, even when they were considering 'policy questions pertaining to the control of crime'; and he gives many examples.

However, following Hirschi, and from a variety of sources of which Gibbs was only one (and not a particularly favourably disposed one), the neglect of the classical concern with effective deterrence has been fully rectified. If interactionism was the leftist response to the inadequacies and failures of positivism, the new deterrence writers represent much more the response of the right (although neither category is ideologically homogeneous). The better-known writers who may be included in this category are Wilson (1975), Van Den Haag (1975) and Ehrlich (1975) in the United States, and Clark (1980) in Britain. Their approaches have been included under the general category of 'administrative criminology' (see Young, 1986), or seen as varieties of control theory (Downes and Rock, 1982). The title 'administrative criminology' is of significance in that it is the title that Vold gave to the classical criminology of Beccaria and Bentham (as we saw in Chapter 1). Thus, the connections with both classicism and control theory have been explicitly recognised.

While recognising a variety of emphases and ideological leanings, Young suggests some common characteristics of these writers: a lack of interest in the causes of crime – or even opposition in the case of proposed *social* causes; a voluntaristic, rather than deterministic, view of human action; a belief in the effectiveness of deterrence. Wilson (1975) specifically relates these new emphases to the failures of positivism. As we have already seen, he noted that positivist criminology had tended to propose causal variables that were difficult, if not impossible to manipulate. He also concluded that in most cases they had simply been wrong. For example, he arrived at the contentious conclusion that the dramatic increase in recorded crime during the period of post-war economic growth in the United States had ruled out poverty and deprivation as being causes of crime.
* These new control theorists have mostly ignored the simplistic classical assumption that 'proportional punishment' will guarantee effective deterrence. Instead, they have concentrated on two main approaches to crime control that they see as appropriate and achievable: increasing the risks and decreasing the opportunities. They have tended to conclude that the most effective method of increasing the risks is by increasing the certainty of detection rather than by increasing the severity of the penalty (but not always; Ehrlich, 1975, is best known

for his advocacy of stiffer penalties, especially the use of capital punishment). Wilson is also an advocate of the particular significance of informal, local community control rather than just more effective policing (these informal controls, it may be remembered, were not considered by the original classical criminologists). The interaction between effective but sensitive community self-surveillance and police surveillance has emerged as perhaps the most favoured approach. Techniques for decreasing the opportunities for crime include such things as the better protection of property, which have been the usual focus of police crime-prevention programmes. Increasing risks and decreasing opportunities tend to be interrelated, of course: better protection and surveillance decrease opportunities by increasing perceived risks. The arguments about the importance of architecture and 'environmental design' in preventing crime that have developed since Newman's (1973) pioneering work, have incorporated a mixture of both these elements (see Hope, 1986, for a useful review of the literature in this area).

This narrowing down of the focus of the original control theory seems to constitute a switch of attention from *offenders* to *situations*. Offenders are assumed to make rational choices (indeed, 'rational choice theory' is now a favoured title for these approaches – see Cornish and Clarke, 1986). Consequently, the offenders are not important; what matters is that opportunities must be reduced and risks increased and this requires that attention be given to the situations in which offences may occur. This is quite different from the original control theory, which was concerned with the differences between individuals in their general dispositions towards offending (based on the strength of their bonds to conformity) and how those differences come about. Hirschi and Gottfredson (1986) have made a useful distinction between these two branches of control theory: the situational approaches constitute explanations of *crime*, while the original control theory is an explanation of *criminality*. That is, the first explain *events* (offences) and the second account for *individual dispositions* (offenders).

Whether Beccaria would have been impressed with these developments is difficult to say: he would probably have liked the logic, practicality and apparent efficiency of the proposals of the situational theorists; like them, he seemed to favour the prevention-is-better-than-cure approach. His own programme was equally narrow in its focus (though different, of course). However, as I suggested in Chapter 1, the basic assumptions of Beccaria's classical model suggest a much wider canvas. He went no further either because of ideological conservatism, or because of lack of courage of his convictions. The new theorists seem to have gone the same way because of ideological conservatism, or fatalism about what is possible. Clearly, these narrower concerns are an important part of classicism, but a fully classical approach has the potential to go much further. As I have already intimated, Hirschi's control perspective seems to me to invite expansion along classical lines, rather than narrowing. Consequently, this is the direction I will be taking in Part Two.

Anti-correctionalism

In the earlier discussion of the background to the emergence of the new sociologists of deviance in the 1960s, one particular theme was mentioned that was not at all compatible with classical criminology: the hostility that the new theorists exhibited to the 'causal-corrective stance'. A discipline devoted to finding out the causes of crime in order that it may be stopped was, they pointed out, uncritically taking up an ideologically committed, conservative stance. For some of the writers this point was taken much further: it was not just a matter of unacknowledged ideological leanings; the causal-corrective stance came to be portrayed as a fundamentally misguided and distorting approach to the study of crime.

The target of this attack was primarily positivist criminology. As we have seen, although positivist criminologists were often shy of associating themselves with specific corrective programmes, they saw crime as pathological and shared a general consensus in favour of a broadly rehabilitative approach to ridding ourselves of it. However, in classical criminology the correctionalist stance was, if anything, more explicit. The mode of correction was, of course, different – reflecting the different assumptions about the nature of human beings: in classical criminology correction is achieved by appeals or threats made to free, rational, choice-making individuals; in positivist criminology it is achieved by altering the variables that *cause* individuals to indulge in criminal behaviour. But this difference does not alter the fundamental similarity in aim; the arguments against correctionalism apply as much to classicism as they do to positivism. Consequently, they must be answered if the potential of the classical perspective is to be developed.

A whole series of arguments against correctionalism can be discerned, originating from various sources, but all gaining impetus in the 1960s and early 1970s: the corrective stance was seen as being inappropriate to an academic discipline in that its partiality had the effect of distorting the nature and appearance of the phenomena it was studying; it was seen as neglecting the possibility that crime may have *positive* qualities and consequences; correctionalism was seen as having led to the violation of fundamental human rights and principles of justice in its single-minded quest for efficient crime control. I will deal with four main forms that these anti-correctionalist arguments have taken.

Correction versus Appreciation

Matza (1969) was particularly influential in proposing that the correctionalist stance had had a distorting effect in criminology, and in advocating an alternative. He argued that correctionalism 'systematically interferes with the capacity to empath-ise and thus comprehend the subject of enquiry' (ibid., p. 15), and consequently increases 'the possibility of "losing the phenomenon" – reducing it to that which it is not' (ibid. p. 17). It is the assumption of pathology that is the root of the problem. The kinds of untruth and distortion that this leads to, he says, stem from the fact that it 'reckons without the patent tenability and durability of deviant enterprise, and without the subjective capacity of man to create novelty and manage diversity' (ibid., p. 44): that is, correctionalism is insensitive to the more positive features of deviance. However, Matza is anxious to avoid romanticising deviance; he sees this as having an equally distorting effect by obscuring 'the seamier and more mundane aspects of the world'. His alternative is what he calls an 'appreciative' stance: 'These appreciative sentiments are easily summarized: we do not for a moment wish that we could rid ourselves of deviant phenomena. We are intrigued by them. They are an intrinsic, ineradicable and vital part of human society' (ibid., p. 17). Despite his opposition to romanticisation, the reference to deviance as being 'vital' clearly suggests that he sees as an established truth that deviance is, to some extent at least, a necessary and positive thing for society. If this can be established as an objective truth, then this would indeed make a correctionalist approach misguided – although only if it were committed to the *total* elimination of deviance. I will be dealing with these kinds of argument, however, in the next subsection.

What seems objectionable in Matza's argument is that he clearly believes there is a 'hierarchy' of stances in relation to deviance, not just alternatives: the appreciative stance is portrayed as superior to either the romantic or the correctionalist in that it is inherently more likely to get at the truth. In analysing this argument, Hirschi (1973, p. 171) concludes that 'Sociology will suffer . . . so long as we believe that our assumptions guarantee truth, while their assumptions guarantee error, whatever the facts may be'. This, however, seems a little unfair to Matza. On a less arrogant interpretation, he seems to be making the reasonable point that the appreciative stance is *less likely to overlook* both positive and negative aspects of deviance simply because it is more open to the acceptance of both possibilities. If we eliminate all ideas of 'guaranteeing' truth or error in any particular approach, this argument seems perfectly acceptable. Matza would clearly be wrong, on the other hand, if he were implying that it was inherently impossible for a corrective stance to acknowledge the 'patent tenability and durability of deviant enterprise'.

In the end, Matza's argument is not so much an attack on correctionalism as an assertion of the not very original point that, whatever your starting assumption, it is best to keep your mind open to all possibilities (although he was right to draw attention to the fact that correctionalists had often been guilty of not doing so). Not only does this mean that you are more likely to get at the truth, but it is also likely to be more fruitful for whatever purpose you have in mind. For example, correctionalists prepared to enter appreciatively into the meaning world of deviants may well come up with something useful for their purposes (although that, of course, is not at all what Matza had in mind).

The Functions of Crime and Deviance

Matza's reference to deviance being 'vital' for society relates to an idea, borrowed from Durkheim, that was popular with the 'new deviance' writers and has played an important part in academic thinking about crime and deviance generally. This is the idea that crime and deviance have positive qualities and consequences that make them *necessary* for the healthy functioning of society. It is easy to see how such a view suited the mood of the period. If crime and deviance could be shown to be vitally necessary then this would be a serious blow indeed to the correctionalist stance – of both positivists and classicists. The arguments amounted to a resurrection of Durkheim's views about the 'functions' of crime. I have argued against these views elsewhere (Roshier, 1977). Since the issue is important to both classical and positivist criminology, I will recapitulate some of the main points here.

The key figure responsible for resurrecting the Durkheimian idea of the functions of crime was Erikson (1966), but it was taken up and used by other writers of the period (for example, Box, 1981). Its Durkheimian origin meant that it suffered at the outset from the more general problems of Durkheim's functionalist approach. The most important of these is that the use of expressions such as 'functional' or 'vitally necessary for society's health' are really ways of disguising value-judgements about what the user finds acceptable or unacceptable in society. This is simply because there are no objective criteria about what constitutes 'health' in a society as there are in the case of biological organisms (such expressions are examples of Durkheim's much-discredited use of biological analogies). But there is no need to revert to these basic objections to functionalism in order to deal with the specific question of the functions of crime.

First, it is necessary to distinguish two quite separate arguments that sometimes seem to get confused: the argument that crime is *inevitable*; and the argument that crime is *functional*. It is obviously the case that showing that something is inevitable is not the same as showing that it is necessary for health and survival. Yet Durkheim himself is responsible for confusing this issue, as well as introducing the suspect assertion of inevitability (see Roshier, 1977, pp. 310–12). But much more important is the assertion of the functions. Two separate ones have been proposed: the 'boundary-maintaining' function, and the 'adaptive' function. The latter is definitely derived from Durkheim. The former is usually associated with him, and Erikson attributes it to him, but in fact it is extremely doubtful whether this is a legitimate interpretation (Roshier, 1977, pp. 310–15).

The boundary-maintaining function, as stated by Erikson, says that crime and the response it evokes provide the essential function of defining and maintaining the moral boundaries of society. Society's need for this is so strong, he says, that it promotes continual and dramatic celebration of deviant acts (originally via public punishments, later via the mass media), and uses inefficient control agencies such as prison in order to produce more, rather than less, crime. The fallacy in this argument, and in other similar versions, is that it confuses the functions of *crime* with the functions of *social control*. It is *social control*, in sanctioning some forms of behaviour and not others, that defines the normative contours of society. The criminal acts themselves contribute nothing to this process since they do not exist as criminal acts unless they have been defined as such by official defining and sanctioning agencies (a point made much of by interactionist writers, including Erikson). A common reply to this is that you cannot have social control without crime or deviance and hence, if social control is necessary, then crime and deviance must be, too. The answer to this, of course, is that if there were no deviance, there would be no need for social control. Social control performs the function of defining those acts that are deemed to be harmful to the society. If such acts did not occur, then neither would social control. The boundary-maintaining function just does not stand up as a function of crime or deviance.

The 'adaptive' function is based on the proposition that what we call crime today includes forms of behaviour that will be crucially necessary to future society – Durkheim's (1938) examples, are the ideas of Socrates and liberal philosophy which were once criminalised but which he sees as vital for contemporary society. The general argument is that the existence of crime ensures sufficient diversity of behaviour and belief to allow society to adapt to new conditions. But proving the necessity of crime requires more than showing that some things that were formerly criminal are now important parts of healthy social life (even if we were to accept that we can objectively determine what constitutes healthy social life). It also requires showing that it was necessary for such behaviour and beliefs to have been *formerly defined as crimes*. If we were to accept that societies need to include a diversity of behaviour and belief in order to adapt to new conditions, this could surely be achieved by simply *allowing* such diversity. It seems perverse, to say the least, to argue that criminalising some forms of behaviour ensures their survival and future usefulness (or, conversely, that *not* criminalising them would guarantee their extinction)!

Arguments such as these for the functional necessity of a category of 'crime' are quite different from arguments that particular activities defined as criminal may in fact be beneficial to society. There may be occasions when we feel ourselves in favour of particular activities that are defined as crimes; but that is entirely different from being in favour of crime. In such cases, the activities are beneficial *in spite of* being defined as crimes, not *because* they are. They are arguments for, if anything, *de*criminalisation. The 'functions' argument is the opposite: it is arguing for the necessity of *criminalisation*. To say that crime is functional and necessary for society's health is to say that we must always ensure that we retain a stock of people whom we humiliate, imprison or (perhaps worst of all) regard as suitable cases for treatment. It is as well that such arguments do not stand up to serious scrutiny.

Socialist Anti-correctionalism

The different sense of 'the functions of crime' – that sometimes what is defined as crime includes activities that some may regard as useful and beneficial – relates to an issue that has long confronted socialists: what is the status of crime and criminals under capitalism? Are they an aspect of the struggle against it? Is correctionalist criminology, of any variety, consequently a part of the ideological superstructure that helps to maintain capitalism? If the answer to these questions is 'yes', then we are back to something rather similar to Durkheim's adaptive function: today's criminals are in fact helping to usher in the better society of tomorrow. To reiterate the point just made, this is not an argument about the functional necessity for all societies to have a category of 'crime' but an argument about the positive qualities of what happens to be defined as crime under capitalism; indeed, the argument is usually combined with the assumption that under socialism there would be no such thing as crime. Nevertheless, since we live in a capitalist society, the argument is an important one for those who would take up a correctionalist stance under it.

The 'new' socialist criminology that emerged from the more politically conscious branch of 1960s interactionism brought this dilemma once again to the forefront. I say 'dilemma' since the 'heroic' view of the criminal under capitalism had always had its problems. Although most socialist writers were agreed that crime resulted from the misery, exploitation, greed and selfishness promoted by the private property relationships of capitalism, they were rather less agreed on the status of the criminal. The fact that 'official' criminals were overwhelmingly from the working class and were seen to be responding to the same forces that promoted socialist consciousness tended to favour at least a positive, if not heroic view of their activities. On the other hand, what they actually *did* was usually very difficult to relate to the requirements of socialist revolution, particularly since it typically victimised its own class rather than capitalists. But to move to the other extreme and regard it as some kind of waste product was to endorse bourgeois correctionalism and, worse still, to acknowledge that the forces that were supposed to produce socialist consciousness could also produce something quite different.

Radzinowicz and Hood (1986) have shown how this dilemma had confronted English socialists from the earliest times. Although Marx and Engels did not systematically apply themselves to crime and its treatment, they too showed some ambivalence in their attitudes to the status of crime under capitalism. According to Radzinowicz and Hood (1986, p. 42), this applied particularly to Engels, who seemed to radically change his mind in the course of his life:

> At first he regarded crime as a form of rebellion among those who had 'courage and passion enough openly to resist society, to reply with declared war upon the bourgeoisie.' But later he stigmatised them as 'the social scum, the passively rotting mass thrown off by the lower layers of the old society.' His final verdict, and in his eyes, the most damaging, was that they were anti-revolutionary. Their crimes were merely a low-grade reflection of the competitive and individualistic element in capitalism; they indulged in an activity which, even in the form of mob violence, could never be effective in the revolutionary movement and, if not crushed, they were more likely to serve as 'part of a bribed tool of reactionary intrigue.' Engels was in no doubt that the lumpenproletariat was 'the worst of all possible allies.' So ended his initial socialist heroic conception of the criminal.

The new socialist criminology of the 1960s and 1970s, however, marked a return to the more romantic view. This was perhaps aided by the fact that the 'criminals' who were the initial focus of attention (counter-culture drug-takers, radical protesters against the Vietnam war and in favour of civil rights) were rather easier to romanticise about. Thus, the two highly influential volumes produced by Taylor, Walton and Young (1973; 1975) espoused a commitment to socialist praxis which opposed both correctionalism and the 'identification of deviance with pathology' (1975, p. 44). Young was later to go through an Engels-like change of heart, though it was clear that he was sceptical from the start (see his contribution to Taylor, Walton and Young, 1975). On the other hand, his early work on Notting Hill drug-takers (1971) exhibited some of the features of what he was later to call 'left idealism'. But there was no ambivalence in other writers: Quinney (1975) insisted that the criminal law must be seen simply as 'a coercive means of enforcing the capitalist social and economic order on an unwilling populace', and added:

> The war against people abroad is part of the same war waged against the oppressed at home . . . A military war is being fought in Asia, while the war on crime with its own weapons is being fought within the USA. All of this to avoid changing the capitalist order, (ibid., p. 200).

Thus was the criminal equated with the Vietcong soldier, the only difference being that the former was struggling against capitalism on the home front.

Fitzgerald (1977, p. 38) criticised the traditional left for not seizing the opportunity of incorporating the prison population as part of the working-class struggle: 'The left, particularly in Britain, has been reluctant to move beyond its traditional insistent focus on the building of the working-class movement and embrace the struggles of minority groups such as prisoners, mental patients, gay liberation.'

Attempts were also made to locate revolutionary potential in the deviant activities of the varieties of working-class youth culture of the period. For example, this was a major theme in the influential collection of essays published by the Centre for Contemporary Cultural Studies (1975). Corrigan and Frith (CCCS, 1975, p. 238) concluded: 'even if youth culture is not political in the sense of being part of a class-conscious struggle for state power, it nevertheless *does provide* a necessary precondition of such a struggle'.

Such ideas were even graced with a 'theory of convergence'. Liebowitz and Horowitz (1968) suggested that what was happening in the United States at the time, was a process of merging of politics and social deviance such that they were becoming indistinguishable. This convergence was, they claimed, occurring from both directions: 'conventional' deviants were organising politically to alter their treatment (prisoners rights organisations, gay liberation, organised ghetto riots) and politically marginal groups were using conventional deviant methods such as robbery and violence to achieve political goals (black power movements, the weathermen, the angry brigade in Britain). Liebowitz and Horowitz were primarily concerned with attacking what they saw as the myopic perspectives of politics and the sociology of deviance, but the clear implication of their convergence thesis was that conventional deviance and leftist political struggle were slowly but surely converging.

Sometimes, however, an alternative, less heroic but equally anti-correctionalist picture was painted: working-class crime was in reality mostly petty, irrelevant and not a problem, but had been made to appear so by the mass media blowing it up, misrepresenting it and creating crime-scares. The reason they do this is to divert attention from the real problem – the crisis of capitalism manifested in economic failure and unrest (see, for example, Hall *et al.*, 1978, on mugging). Rises in crime are thus, in reality, rises in criminalisation by the state's agents (the police) prompted by the requirement for diversionary scapegoats.

Meanwhile, the 'real' criminals were defined as being capitalism's large corporations and state agencies. They were seen as being responsible for the real problems that confront ordinary citizens. Because of their dominant power position, however, they were able to avoid such actions being defined as crimes or, where they were (for the purpose of ideological mystification), they were deliberately ineffectively sanctioned. For this reason, one of the major spin-offs of left idealism was a resurgence of interest in the sociology of law, concerned with how the legal rules that define crimes come about and serve the changing requirements of capitalism (see Young, 1986, p. 17).

These arguments amounted to a double attack on correctionalism. On the one hand the 'official' crime that correctionalists were bent on correcting was either authentic working-class rebellion or an irrelevance blown up out of all proportion by the agents of capitalism for their own malevolent purposes. On the other hand the 'real' crime that *did* need correcting was being perpetrated by the capitalists themselves (and those very same agents), and was being ignored.

An important point to note here is that these were not really arguments against correctionalism as such. Rather, they were arguments about the *focus* of correctionalism: that the definitions of crime, the supposed causes and supposed cures were all wrong. Interestingly, while for positivist criminologists the causes of and cures for crime were matters that always needed 'more research', for left idealists they needed no research at all – they were already clearly known: crime was caused by the inequalities and degradations of capitalism, and was cured by the transition to socialism. It was not simply a matter of switching the definitions of crime from what the working class do to what the capitalist class do (that would merely be a transitional strategy); in the socialist society both upper- and lower-class crime would disappear since there would be 'a set of social arrangements in which there would be no politically, economically and socially-induced need to criminalise deviance' (Taylor, Walton and Young, 1973, p. 270).

For these reasons, however, left idealism constitutes a very serious attack on correctionalism *under capitalism*. If the arguments are correct, then involving oneself with correctionalism is an act of commitment to pro-capitalist, conservative ideology. Correctionalist criminologists, of all varieties, join all the other agents of social control that capitalism utilises to patch itself up and keep its exploitative machinations justified and operational.

There are several crucial assumptions in the left idealist position. First, and most important, there are its assumptions about the nature and meaning of working-class crime; second, the view that 'real' crime is located in the activities of the ruling class; and finally, there is its particular version of the causes of and cures for crime. The last point will be taken up, in a wider context, in Chapter 7. The other two require some attention here.

The better documented of the two is the second idea of 'ruling-class' crime. There has undoubtedly been a remarkable increase in research and literature in this area, stimulated by left idealist and other post-interactionist writers, although the pioneer work had been done much earlier by Sutherland (1945). This new interest has not relied simply on a moral redefinition of 'crime' to draw attention to analogous, but uncriminalised, activities of the ruling class (although that has been part of it). Much work has centred on activities that *are* criminal, by contemporary definitions, but are hidden and undetected – one of the greatest benefits of power being the privacy and impunity that it seems to guarantee (see Geis and Stotland, 1980). On the face of it, however, this does not seem to favour an anti-correctionalist position, but rather a redirection of its focus from lower- to upper-class crime. But that would be to ignore the taken-for-granted causal-corrective argument of left idealism: that ruling-class crime, like so-called working-class crime, can *only* be eliminated by the transition to socialism; anything else would be useless tinkering. However, if this is not taken as proven, and if everything is not to be left to the socialist revolution, the evidence about ruling-class crime suggests, if anything, an *extension* of the scope of correctionalist criminology rather than its rejection.

Returning to the first assumption of left idealism – the interpretation of the ideological nature of working-class crime – here we are presented with much greater difficulties. Even if working-class crime *is* promoted by the same features of capitalism as produce socialist consciousness this is no basis for automatically equating them: working-class crime may express purely personal goals or, if there are some wider underlying objectives, they cannot necessarily be assumed to be socialist ones. With the exception of deeply divided societies such as Northern Ireland, it has tended in practice to be very difficult to attribute more than the most limited amount of crime to *any* kind of underlying ideological commitment. For example, even in the relatively active period in which Liebowitz and Horowitz were writing, only a minute proportion of *total* crime could conceivably be attributed to marginal political groups' expressing themselves in conventional criminal activity.

But perhaps it is asking too much to expect some sort of articulated political goal – especially of the young adolescents who are responsible for the bulk of working-class crime. As Corrigan and Frith (1975) suggested, we should really be looking at the *potential* that is expressed in their deviant lifestyles and 'resistance' activities. The problem here, however, is what counts as potential, and what is it potential of? Not surprisingly, left idealist writers have been very reluctant to identify anything as being other than potentially indicative of leftist revolutionary consciousness. A good example of the problems this can create was Pearson's (1976) study of 'Paki-bashing' by working-class youths in Accrington. On the face of it, such activity would seem to be more expressive of right-wing rather than left-wing sentiments. Yet Pearson specifically rejected this interpretation by arguing that, in the context of the insecure industrial history of Accrington, such behaviour could be seen as an understandable response although not, of course, one to be approved of. But this seems to be an extremely dangerous conclusion from the point of view of a leftist interpretation. The most obvious conclusion to be drawn from his study, although not at all what he intended, was that an embryonic rightist consciousness may emerge as an authentic, meaningful response to the contradictions of capitalism. But Pearson does not allow this: it is a 'false' response generated by the capitalist media. He falls back on the popular device for explaining why the working class fail to live up to what is expected of them – they are reduced to mindless automatons, responding only to right-wing media messages.

The relative success of right-wing organisations, compared with left-wing ones, in recruiting among lower-class youth culture has always been a problem for left idealism. Robins and Cohen (1978) provide the sad and honest tale of an attempt to work with and politicise working-class youths in a working-class area of London. They were constantly overwhelmed by racist, anti-radical attitudes and by the much greater appeal of the National Front. But, once again, they are loath to recognise this as a *real* and alternative response to the conditions confronting lower-class youth. Rather, it is seen as something having gone wrong: corruption by the 'commercial entrepreneurs of youth fashion' and 'social disorganisation' makes them 'vulnerable' to right-wing populism and racism (ibid., pp. 171–2). Thus they replace positivist criminology's pathological view of working-class crime with a pathological view of working-class criminals' ideology.

The nature of the impicit political ideology of criminals is well illustrated when we consider what happens when they become organised and powerful, as in the case of the Mafia in the United States, and the smaller-scale, localised organisations that have appeared in some of our cities. In these circumstances they are more able to realise their true ideological potential, which seems to mean taking on the characteristics of the most rapacious forms of capitalist entrepreneurship. As Packer (1968) has pointed out, the criminality of their enterprise acts as a kind of 'tariff' that protects them from the competition of 'legitimate' entrepeneurs unwilling to take the risks of illegal enterprise, and provides them with customers who have no legal redress against the most excessive forms of exploitation. In almost every respect they represent the exact antithesis of the spirit of socialist collectivism.

The burgeoning of leftist idealism in the 1970s was, however, opposed from within the ranks of the left from the start. Hirst (1975), for example, was a particular opponent of the position of Taylor, Walton and Young on various grounds. He was particularly scathing of any suggestion of romanticisation, invoking the later, revised view of Engels of criminals as parasites on their own class and ideologically and politically at odds with the worker's movement towards socialism.

The weaker version of left idealism – that working-class crime is an irrelevance, dramatised by the capitalist media for diversionary purposes – has had an important resurgence in the 1980s with reference to black urban crime, thus adding a racial component to the original class issue (see Tierney, 1988, for both an analysis and an evocation of the sense of *déjà vu*). Here the argument is that correctionalists are helping to divert attention away from the 'real' problems, rather than that they are necessarily helping to crush revolutionary potential. This view has been powerfully opposed under the title of 'socialist realism', principally espoused by Jock Young, now fully divested of whatever idealist tendencies he may have had in his Taylor, Walton and Young days (Lea and Young, 1984; Matthews and Young, 1986).

Armed with the poweful empirical evidence of the Islington Crime Survey (Jones, MacLean and Young, 1986), socialist realism challenges the view that working-class crime is a non-problem which does not deserve the attention of left-thinking criminologists. In doing so it has been heaped with opprobrium by other sections of the left (see Kettle, 1984). The Crime Survey is a victimisation study and its main conclusion is one that has been noted, in a less systematic way, many times before: working-class crime *is* a problem, and it is a problem *for the working class*, since they are its principal victims, as they are of all types of crime:

> Crime is not an activity of latter day Robin Hoods – the vast majority of working class crime is directed within the working class. It is intra-class *not* inter-class in its nature . . . Crimes of violence, for example, are by and large one poor person hitting another poor person – and in almost half these instances it is a man hitting his wife or lover . . . the more vulnerable a person is economically and socially the more likely it is that *both* working class and white-collar crime will occur against them (Matthews and Young, 1986, p. 23).

As a result, socialist realism espouses a new interest in correctionalism – even under capitalism.

Left idealism has badly misrepresented the nature and meaning of crime and has failed in its dismissal of correctionalism. However, it did draw attention to an important point that seemed to have eluded positivist correctionalism: crime does not have a blanket, objective status that enables us automatically to be against it regardless of what 'it' is. In this respect it does have an important message for correctionalism. *Crime is a moral and political category. The nature, and application, of the legal rules that define crime, together with the moral and political debate that their consideration inevitably involves, is as important for correctionalism as for any other criminological enterprise.* To a limited and inadequate extent this *was* recognised in classical criminology: Beccaria acknowledged that the *content*, as well as the operation, of legal rules was likely to be a significant factor in the degree of compliance that could be expected. Positivist criminology, on the other hand, seemed scarcely to recognise it at all.

Correctionalism and Injustice

It was noted in Chapter 1 that attempts in the early nineteenth century to put Beccaria's classical programme into practice encountered severe difficulties: the desire to make punishment solely concerned with effective deterrence, rather than with equating suffering with desert, proved to be unacceptable on the grounds of its retributive injustice. The result was the uneasy compromise between deterrent and retributive aims that characterised neoclassicism. The twentieth-century advance of rehabilitation as a penal aim, which was favoured by positivist criminologists, also attempted to exclude retributive considerations of desert from penal treatment. Ultimately, it too was to be opposed, on the same grounds. The charge of inherent injustice represents yet another attack on correctionalism, in whatever guise it appears.

The problem was essentially the same for both classical deterrence and rehabilitation, despite their different aims: there was no *necessary* relationship between either the amount of deterrent punishment or the amount of rehabilitation required to deter or cure particular criminals, and the gravity of their offences. As penal aims, they both led to injustice in retributive terms. However, as we have seen, Beccaria avoided the main confrontation with retribution by making the totally unwarranted assumption that the most effective deterrents *would* be those that equated punishments with offences. By a different route, he arrived at the same conclusion of 'proportionality' as retribution required. But he also wished to exclude from consideration all 'mitigating' factors, such as the personal characteristics of the offender and the circumstances of the offence, since he saw these as irrelevant to effective deterrence (as was the concept of 'mitigation' itself). Consequently, the end result was still a serious violation of retributive justice.

Rehabilitation represented a much more comprehensive rejection of retributive justice. The fact that it also rejects punishment in favour of individualised treatment geared to the particular needs of the offender has meant that, unlike deterrence, it has managed to present itself as a humane, caring alternative to the 'primitive revenge' of retribution. Indeed, since the claim is that punishment does not happen, questions of 'proportionality' simply do not arise. Yet, alongside the other rebellions of the 1960s and 1970s, rehabilitation has been the subject of virulent attack – and precisely on the grounds of its actual inhumanity, as well as its injustice and hypocrisy. I will briefly outline the nature of this reaction, and then consider its implications for classical criminology.

We saw in Chapter 1 that, in Britain, there is some dispute as to when rehabilitation began to make serious inroads into penal practice: Foucault saw it as manifesting itself in the rise of the prison as the dominant penal institution; Garland puts it much later, in the early part of this century. But either way, by the 1960s there was an extraordinarily wide and established consensus among penal administrators about the primacy of rehabilitative aims. Conrad (1965, pp. 12–13), in his interesting study of penal practice in nine different European countries, was able to come up with five postulates shared by penal administrators in all of them; and they spell out precisely the rehabilitative programme:

(1) Offenders are social deviates; something is wrong with them.
(2) Punishment exacted by the system is futile. Commitment to the system is punishment enough.
(3) During the period of commitment the correctional agency has an obligation to administer a regime which will equip offenders to 'lead a good and useful life on discharge'.
(4) Because the treatment required by the offender varies from individual to individual in accordance with what is 'wrong' with each, the duration and circumstances of the commitment must also vary.
(5) All correctional agencies have the obligation to maintain control over committed offenders.

Conrad rightly emphasises that this was a consensus about what *should be* happening. What *was* happening was rather different. Nor did the consensus extend much beyond ranks of penal administrators (or even to their immediate subordinates, as Conrad noted). The overall picture of sentencing and penal practice presents a rather more complicated situation. I think it can be summarised in the following way: it incorporates penal treatments with different aims; deterrent (fines), rehabilitative (probation), deterrent and rehabilitative (prison), and so on; for sentencing purposes these different treatments are arranged in a notional 'tariff' system which equates the gravity of the offence and the culpability of the offender with the seriousness of the treatment. In other words, rehabilitation has been added as another complication to the already compromised neoclassical position which, as we have already seen, has dominated most Western systems since the early part of the last century: the dominant operational framework is still the retributive tariff. The most quantitatively significant development in terms of *content* this century has not been rehabilitation but deterrence (through the massive expansion in the use of the fine, as we saw in Chapter 2).

However, rehabilitation has made rather more significant inroads than is suggested by the formal description of the system. This is because the sentence itself only partly determines what happens to offenders. For example, the length of time offenders spend in institutions is not decided by the sentence. Prisoners can be released, on parole, after serving only one-third of their sentence; the decision is made on rehabilitative grounds – the offender is released when considered 'cured' and safe. Similarly, for juvenile offenders, the 'care order' under which they may be detained in an institution is for an unspecified period; again, release is determined by rehabilitative, treatment criteria. Borstal, too (now abandoned), was an 'indeterminate' sentence. In some jurisdictions (for example, Scotland) juvenile offenders are dealt with almost entirely under civil rather than criminal proceedings; in others, including the English, this is partly the case. Under civil proceedings, the appropriate care and cure of the young offender is, in theory at least, the only consideration.

Most academic criminologists had tended to regard the advances of rehabilitation in the penal process as being a beneficial and humane trend. But in the late 1960s and early 1970s there was a marked turn of the tide. Starting in those countries where the rehabilitative approach had progressed furthest, the United States (see the American Friends Service Committee, 1971), and Scandinavia (see Christie, 1974) this reversal of opinion soon established itself in Britain (see Bean, 1976; Hood, 1978; Taylor, Lacey and Bracken, 1980). All of these studies emphasised the same, fundamental point: that rehabilitation had led to the sacrifice of justice in favour of an alternative goal that it had manifestly failed to achieve.

First it was pointed out that, whatever the *intention*, rehabilitation does punish people; in particular, it allows people to be put into institutions where they would rather not be. More importantly, it puts them there for indeterminate periods (until they are 'cured') which can, and does, mean longer than would be warranted by retributive justice (determined by the gravity of their offence). Also, it was argued that the 'relaxation' of the criminal process for juveniles in practice often means simply the abandonment of the safeguards guaranteed by the 'due process' of law, and a slipshod approach to, for example, the vital matter of guilt determination. Finally, the abandonment of desert in favour of individual diagnosis and treatment justified treating people with the same offence and record entirely differently, leaving it wide open to bias – especially in terms of social class. This is particularly the case in relation to juveniles, since there is a heavy reliance on family background characteristics as indicators of treatment need, which themselves are likely to be class-related (see Roshier and Teff, 1980, pp. 140–1).

These problems would be serious enough even if the rehabilitative approach were demonstrably successful in 'curing' crime. But perhaps the greatest source of its downfall was the fact that there was no evidence that it was. Despite some early false claims, properly controlled studies of various rehabilitative programmes invariably concluded that they were no more (and no less) successful than their alternatives in preventing reconvictions (see Hood and Sparks, 1970). In the course of the 1970s various 'summary' analyses of large numbers of 'effectiveness' studies – Lipton, Martinson and Wilks (1975) and Brody (1976) being perhaps the best known – came to the same negative conclusion. When combined with the growing criticisms of its injustice, these findings undermined all the claims for enlightenment and scientific efficiency that had been made for rehabilitation as a penal aim.

Rehabilitation is another manifestation of positivism which was under general attack at this time. In some ways it represents its worst dehumanising features – the reduction of meaningful human action to a kind of technical fault (based on the medical analogy) to be cured by applied technology. A common theme in the reaction against it has been a demand for the 'return to justice': retributive justice is seen as having the virtue of acknowledging that it is punishing 'responsible' people, which in turn requires the safeguards of individual rights and public accountability of the 'due process of law', and the limitations on intervention in people's lives provided by the principle of retributive proportionality.

Von Hirsch (1983) has noted that this disenchantment with rehabilitation and the revival of the concern with justice and proportionality have been quite wrongly labelled as a revival of classicism. This is probably due to confusion caused by Beccaria's advocacy of proportionality: his version, of course, specifically excluded any concern with justice and desert. In fact, the arguments about the injustice of rehabilitation apply equally to classical criminology's advocacy of efficient deterrence. Beccaria's assumption of the special effectiveness of proportional deterrence is unsubstantiated. The same analyses that have undermined rehabilitation have also undermined some classical deterrent assumptions: the evidence does not suggest that more punishment automatically provides more deterrence or that more serious crimes necessarily require more punishment to deter them. Effective deterrence, if there is such a thing, is just as likely to violate retributive justice and proportionality as rehabilitation does.

The revived concern for retributive justice has not been the only response to the failure of the rehabilitative ideal. As we saw in the earlier section on control theory, there has been a new interest in deterrence and prevention as well, attempting to improve on the original, crude formulations of Beccaria. There have also been attempts to promote more humane-looking alternatives such as restitution and reconciliation (for example, Wright, 1982). The problem with the 'return to justice' is the same problem that classical criminology reacted against: retributive justice seems pointless and irrational; it has no practical objectives in relation to crime – unlike deterrence, rehabilitation, restitution and reconciliation. Yet, at the same time, practical programmes that ignore justice in retributive terms are not only likely to prove unacceptable, but are also likely to be self-defeating: the sense of injustice that they generate militates against the effectiveness of their programmes. The incompatibility of justice and correction as penal objectives has long been, and still remains, the major unsolved problem of penal practice and consequently remains a major issue for the correctionalist stance in criminology. I will return to it again in Chapter 8. But, briefly, a concluding point needs to be made here about the way classical criminology relates to this dilemma.

I have suggested that although Beccaria selected deterrence as his mode of crime control, his arguments invite other possibilities. His primary commitment was to effective control; he chose deterrence because it seemed most obviously to follow from his views on human rationality. But he acknowledged that, for example, education could achieve the same objectives. Thus, one of the main tenets of rehabilitation (faith in education) was also comptatible with classical criminology. However, this hardly helps with the problem of retributive justice, of which Beccaria was particuarly dismissive. But again, there is the other side to Beccaria's version of the social contract mentioned in Chapter 1 – that we would not will for others what we would not will for ourselves – and Hart's view that Beccaria's position was sensitive to individual rights. Both allow that the individual's sense of justice is an important consideration both for its own sake and for the sense of commitment to the social contract that is as important for controlling crime as was deterrence. As we saw in Chapter 1, there are unresolved conflicts between Beccaria's fundamental assumptions about the nature of human beings, the social contract and the functions of punishment, on the one hand, and the particular mode of control that he derives from them, on the other. A coherent classical position by no means precludes the issue of retributive justice. Consequently, an attempt will be made to reconcile justice and correction in the postclassical perspective put forward in Part Two (in Chapter 8).

Conclusion

This chapter has given more space to the anti- rather than to the pro-classical themes that emerged in the 1960s and 1970s. But this is not representative of the balance between them. My general conclusion is that the pro-classical themes are the more important: they have opened up the opportunity for an extensive development of the unnecessarily narrow focus of Beccaria's original formulation of classical criminology, and this opportunity will be taken up in Part Two.

The general attacks on positivism since the 1960s, together with the various dismissals of correctionalism that have been associated with them, have had the effect of virtually eclipsing the traditional causal-corrective concern of criminology. As Young (1986) has pointed out, we seem to be left only with the practical but extremely narrow focus of the new 'administrative' criminologists, or the unexamined, taken-for-granted (and contradictory) explanations of 'left idealism'. The attacks on correctionalism are particularly important here since, as I have stressed throughout, they apply equally (if they apply at all) to classical criminology. I have argued that correctionalism is no more inherently flawed than any other starting assumption (including 'appreciation') that the alleged functions of crime are a myth, and that socialist anti-correctionalism is really nothing of the sort, but an argument about the nature of officially defined crime (though it rightly draws attention to the fact that correctionalism cannot justifiably avoid such an argument). The relationship between justice and classical correctionalism, it was concluded, raises some long-term, complex issues which will require further consideration later.

PART TWO

Postclassical Criminology

Introduction

In Part One I have briefly outlined the origins and fate of the classical perspective in criminology. It seems to have finally resolved itself into an increased interest in practical deterrence and street-level prevention programmes. While such concerns are admirable in their no-nonsense practicality, they represent a significant decline in ambition when compared with the other criminologies that have appeared during the two hundred years that have passed since Beccaria wrote. To use Hirschi and Gottfredson's (1986) terminology, there seems to have been a retreat from explanations of *criminality*, to explanations of *crime* – from explaining criminal dispositions, to explaining (or rather preventing) criminal acts. It could be argued, and indeed is, that since the more ambitious criminologies of the past are mostly in ruins, this new modesty and realism are a welcome change. Others, including myself, share the feelings of Young (1986) that this purely 'administrative' criminology is a poor thing – anti-theoretical, unrelated to wider social contexts, and depoliticised.

It can be perfectly reasonably claimed that this current heir of classicism owes much to the original: we saw, in Chapter 1, that Beccaria's focus was equally practical and almost as narrow. However, I have argued that this need not be so; the classical perspective, in the basic form laid down by Beccaria, has much greater potential than has been exploited so far. In Part Two I want to try to develop some of this potential and outline a 'postclassical' perspective: that is, a perspective grounded on the fundamental assumptions made by Beccaria, but with some liberties taken and adjustments made in the light of the various problems it has encountered. But first, in looking at the history of classical principles in the previous chapters I have left loose ends untied and contradictions unresolved. It may help to summarise briefly the current position.

I have suggested that classical criminology can be formulated in terms of some basic assumptions about the nature of human beings and of criminal action. Three were selected as the most important: freedom, rationality and manipulability. But Beccaria took a narrow view of how to manipulate the human tendency freely and rationally to choose deviation: he saw it only in terms of the effectiveness of the operations of the criminal justice system. In addition, he only considered those operations in terms of deterrence, and ignored such vital factors as the practical (as well as the moral) consequences of abandoning retributive justice.

Positivist criminology has failed in its avowed intention to replace classical criminology with an objective, scientific model of the causes and treatment of crime. It has failed to establish clear-cut causal variables that differentiate offenders from non-offenders, and failed to specify effective individualised treatment programmes. The best it has been able to achieve is loose, probabilistic associations which sometimes, in all but the terminology used, have treated individual offenders as at least partially free, rational and choice-making (and in so doing, has to some extent converged with classical criminology). Positivist criminology's almost complete abandonment of the classical concern with the significance of the criminal justice system has been a serious omission.

The 1960s and 1970s witnessed the reappearance and redirection of some classical themes. Interactionism reinstated the voluntarism of human action and the focus on crime rather than the criminal. In the latter case, however, it emphasised the crime-producing rather than the crime-controlling features of the criminal justice system. It also pointed to an important development that can and should be expected of the classical perspective: the assertion of the relativity and selectivity of criminal definitions and their application. However, interactionism became predominantly associated with 'labelling theory' which, as we saw, tended to revert to the status of another (and suspect) positivist-type causal theory.

At about the same time, control theory emerged, utilising similar basic assumptions to those of classical criminology, despite being located in the positivist tradition. Its contribution was to concentrate on factors *outside* of the criminal justice system that control the natural human tendency towards deviance. However, even in Hirschi's formulation, the social context that was considered was a fairly narrow one and, in subsequent developments, became narrower still. Nevertheless, in conjunction with the classical themes of interactionism, it seemed to offer the basis for a new, resurgent classical criminology.

But this has not happened. The main developments since interactionism have been in phenomenological, Marxist and feminist sociology. The first two of these have, for different reasons, dissociated themselves from the causal-corrective concerns of traditional criminology. Phenomenological sociology, with its micro-level focus on human meaning construction, has mostly ruled out any specific interest in substantive areas of human action such as crime. For Marxist sociology, as we have seen, cause and correction have not usually been problematic, since capitalism has been assumed to be the cause and the transition to socialism the cure; their attention has been more directed to capitalist law-creation and -enforcement. Feminist sociology, on the other hand, in its critique of the male-centred character of all previous criminology, *has* involved itself with the traditional criminological concerns.

The 'postclassical' criminology I have in mind needs to bring together and develop these various 'lost' strands of classicism. It requires a wider view of both the *sources* of control and the *contexts* in which they operate, and must be applicable to more than just male working-class crime. This is the task of Part Two.

4 Assumptions and Definitions

The particular starting assumptions by which I have characterised classical criminology in Chapter 1 concern the nature of human beings and their relationship with crime and conformity. These assumptions require some reconsideration as a starting point for the development of the postclassical perspective.

The issues I will be discussing are ones that have engaged philosophers for many hundreds of years and on which a vast literature has accumulated. Consequently, it would be unrealistic, not to mention arrogant, to suppose that I am likely to make any new contribution to them. In which case, it seems worth asking why I am considering them at all within the limited confines of this book. The answer to that, I think, is fairly straightforward: they are issues on which some position *has* to be taken; if the position is not spelled out it is still nevertheless there, implicitly guiding the way the work is conducted. I think this has been well illustrated in the previous chapters – particularly in the case of positivist criminology. Not spelling your position out does have some advantages – it leaves your options slightly more open in the event of future attacks. But it has the disadvantage of confusion and obscurantism.

In what follows I will not be proposing solutions so much as ways of working with these problems in relation to the study of crime and its correction. They are ways which, in the light of the previous two hundred years of intellectual engagement with these areas, seem to me to be the most fruitful.

Freedom and Manipulability

In the conclusion to Chapter 2, I suggested that the gulf between the view of humans as free and choice-making, on the one hand, and determined by forces outside of their control, on the other, may not be as unbridgeable as it seems. In the study of crime, particularly with respect to its predictability (and manipulability, which I will be looking at next), the more moderate versions of these two positions have shown some potentiality for convergence. I pointed out that in practice determinist theories have always had to acknowledge a low level of predictive power for their causal variables. In determinist terms, this is explained by the virtually infinite complexity of different constellations of different causal variables in individual cases. *In principle* these constellations are knowable, and criminal behaviour fully predictable. *In practice* it is always out of the question: there is always a residuum of unpredictability. Similarly, moderate versions of indeterminism (especially the classical version) allow a degree of predictability: although we are seen as making free choices, this does not preclude the specification of circumstances that influence choices in a particular direction. But again, there is always a residuum of unpredictability; we can always opt to choose not to be influenced in the predicted direction.

'Practical' determinism and 'practical' indeterminism thus converge in allowing that circumstances can be specified which give rise to varying levels of probability of crime occurring. And they both acknowledge the inevitability of a residuum of unpredictability. The main difference is in the language used to describe what is responsible for that residuum: for determinists it is the variability of constellations of causes in individual cases; for indeterminists it is our ability to choose not to be predictable.

Which language should be used by postclassical criminology? Its name and original allegiance suggests the indeterminist. And there is another reason that would favour it: the language of free choice is the language that is used in everyday life by the people it purports to describe. However, there is a debit side as well: how do we know when we have reached the limits of predictability and 'bottomed out' on the residuum of free choice? Matza (1964), whose 'soft determinist' position approximates the one under consideration, shows how arbitrary the answer to this question can be – in his case it seems to be when you have finished reading his book! The determinist position, with its assumption that the complexity of causes is at least *potentially* discoverable, avoids such arbitrary cut-off points and fires researchers continually to attempt to improve their predictive effectiveness (a point made by Hook, cited, but not heeded, by Matza, 1964, pp. 10–11). Heuristically, determinism seems to have the advantage. So the answer seems to be: *talk* like an indeterminist, *act* like a determinist.

The argument about the convergence of moderate determinism and moderate indeterminism in their positions on the predictability of criminal action, applies equally to their positions on manipulability. Again, the difference between them is in the language used to describe this process: for determinists manipulation is achieved by altering the factors that cause criminal behaviour; for indeterminists it is achieved by making crime a relatively less attractive choice. And once again I would propose that the language of indeterminism is preferable: it portrays human action as an expression of motives, reasons and purposes open to the influence of incentives and disincentives in a way that 'makes sense' to us as potential offenders ourselves. I am not suggesting that it is proven that our motives, reasons and purposes are not themselves reducible to mechanically operating causal factors, as a fully determinist model would have it; but if that *is* the case, we are so far from being able to specify these factors that they do not offer a model we can actually work with – as we saw in the discussion of positivist criminology in Chapter 2.

Postclassical criminology, then, sees criminal action as chosen and as expressing the purposes, intentions, and meanings attached to the situations in which it occurs, of those who indulge in it. But these choices are not seen as being so individually idiosyncratic as to make crime totally unpredictable or uncontrollable. It is assumed that there is sufficient uniformity to facilitate the specification of situations and circumstances that make it more, or less, likely to occur. These situations and circumstances are not seen as operating as 'causes', in a determinist sense, but as offering incentives or disincentives that will have some degree of probability of influencing the direction in which the choices are made.

Finally, the concern with manipulation means that postclassical criminology is correctionalist, as were its classical and positivist predecessors; that is why I have spent some time, in Chapter 3, countering anti-correctionalist arguments. Crime, in the postclassical perspective, is seen as undesirable – something that, as far as possible, we could do without. But this does not mean that it takes the conservative stance of necessarily accepting existing definitions of crime. Quite the contrary, it assumes that *the nature of criminal definitions and their application are factors that influence people's decisions whether to comply with them or not*, and are therefore an issue for correctionalism. The moral debate about what should be defined as crime is a debate about what we think is undesirable, and should not therefore be tolerated. Crime cannot be controlled without confronting the issue of what should be crime; and to say what should be crime is to say what should be controlled.

Rationality and Criminal Motivation

If human action expresses motives and purposes, a question that arises is where the motives for *criminal* action come from (especially if we are unable to specify their 'causes', in the positivist sense). The classical answer is simply that they are there; they are taken as given. They are part of the conception of human rationality which, as we saw in Chapter 1, is one of the starting assumptions of classical criminology. Our dominant motivations are those of rational self-interest and they tend to lead us into crime because crime, however defined, involves self-restraint. So, in classical terms, our rationality makes us 'naturally' criminal.

However, I have stressed the importance of the other side of our self-interested rationality – the side that also enables us to appreciate the personal advantages to be gained from compliance with the restraints of the social contract. In Chapter 1 I suggested that these two sides to our rational self-interestedness imply that we have an ambiguous, fluctuating relationship with whatever is defined as crime and conformity. In 'postclassical criminology' I want to emphasise this ambiguity much more. In particular, I am interpreting it to imply that we are not simply governed by considerations of immediate personal advantage. We will also be more prepared (though by no means certain) to comply with personal constraints under two conditions: that the constraints are seen as being in the service of some greater 'good' and that they are seen as operating justly and fairly. This allows a much more complicated picture of our relationship with crime and conformity than that proposed by the simple deterrence of Beccaria's classical criminology, or the cause–effect of positivism. There are different considerations, often pulling in different directions. It also means a more complicated view of humans than the interpretation that is often put on the classical conception – that we are 'naturally evil'. In the postclassical view, we are *both* 'evil' and 'good' (however these are socially defined); the same people are capable of either. The 'natural' deviance that is taken for granted as a human capability in the postclassical perspective is precisely that – a capability, not an inevitability.

Although this postclassical perspective contains some important modifications of the original classical position, it still retains its essential spirit as an explanatory framework. Deviant motivations, for example, are still taken as given; it is conformity rather than deviance that remains problematic. This is because, despite the partial retreat from the more uniformly selfish version of humans in the original classical position, the postclassical view still also retains Beccaria's vision of the uneasy relationship between 'private passions' and the 'common good'. Both of these expressions, however, have rather different underlying assumptions. Private passions are not assumed to be a universal, biologically determined category (they are of unknown origin, not assumed to be necessarily identical across different cultures). Similarly, the common good (or rather, that part of it defined by legal rules) is not taken to be an objective category. It is a common good defined by those who have been in a position to define it as such (through their access to the processes that determine the nature of legal rules). Yet, despite this relativistic view of both private passions and the common good, the inevitability of a tension between them – of the problematic nature of conformity to the common good rather than deviation – is retained. This point will be elaborated further in the discussion of 'crime' in the next section.

The postclassical version of human rationality and motivation can perhaps be illustrated by taking a simple example – my relationship with the laws against speeding when I am driving home late at night. I generally approve of this restraint – I see it as serving some greater 'good' and, on the whole, as being applied reasonably fairly. I have relatively high stakes in conformity – I happen to have done fairly well out of it; I would have a certain amount to lose in terms of reputation were I to be apprehended. On the other hand, I do not have *that* much to lose – speeding, in our culture at least, does not carry all that much stigma (even in the section of it that I inhabit). Also, as it is late with few people around, I see the dangers to others of my speeding as being less. But I also acknowledge that such exceptions cannot be realistically incorporated into the application of such rules. At the same time, my sense of impunity is high – there are few police around and it would be easy to spot them if they were; the risk in terms of the formal sanction (probably a fine and endorsement) are consequently low. And I would gain considerable advantage from speeding; I am tired and I want to get home to bed. I am not suggesting that all such considerations are rationally run through and weighed up on every occasion; they are too familiar to require it. But the elements (both dispositional and situational) are variable – according to the particular person involved and the particular circumstances.

Although the above example is a relatively trivial one, it is the kind of image of our imprecise and variable relationship with crime and conformity that I wish to portray in postclassical criminology. Later I will be trying to explore some of the factors which influence our dispositions towards whether or not to commit crimes. First, however, there are some objections to the starting assumption of our 'natural' criminality that require some attention. Some of these are tied up with the conception of crime itself, and will be dealt with in the next section. But there are others that must be dealt with here.

Taking criminal motivations as 'given' seems a rather glib way of dealing with them. It excludes them from consideration – not, of course, because they play no part in accounting for crime (quite the opposite, they are the essential prerequisite). But it appears to imply that we are all equally disposed to crime all the time; there are no individual differences in motivation; variations in individual criminal *action* are solely accounted for by variations in the constellations of incentives and disincentives that apply in each case.

This is not how I conceive of the situation in postclassical criminology. Differences in motivation between individuals, and during individuals' life-spans, and for different kinds of crime, are acknowledged. *But individual differences are seen as relatively much less significant in accounting for variations in criminal action between different individuals, different groups, and over different time-periods than are variations in the control exercised by perceived incentives and disincentives.* Essentially, postclassical criminology sees crime as best accounted for in terms of the factors that influence the likelihood of 'given' motives being translated into action. Once again, it is purely a matter of heuristic fruitfulness. The argument is that the postclassical perspective is a relatively more useful one for accounting for, and understanding the manipulation of, criminal action.

The prevalence of criminal motivations is not too difficult to accept in the case of examples such as that of speeding, used above. But in other categories, it becomes rather more difficult to convince people that it is a potentiality of most of us and that no 'special' motivation is required to explain it. Some time ago, Matza and Sykes (1961) suggested that this is because among 'respectable' people criminal motivations exist at the 'subterranean' level and only surface on special, licensing situations such as the business man's night on the town, carnivals, office parties, student rags, and so on. Alternatively, they are expressed vicariously through tastes in films and television. An interesting example of the latter would be vandalism – often picked on as being a particularly 'inexplicable' activity in conventional motivational terms; yet in the early years of the film industry the destruction of property (especially the most prized objects such as cars) constituted the most popular film content, and still draws large audiences today.

Fiction and drama, when they are done well and provide a convincing, realistic context in which serious crimes occur, can often enable us to imagine ourselves doing things which, in the abstract description, we would consider impossible. Also, real contexts such as wars or urban riots provide innumerable examples of 'ordinary' people doing things that would be unimaginable of them in more conventional contexts.

Veblen (1922, p. 237), in his 'theory of the leisure class', has drawn attention to the fact that it would be difficult to argue that we are 'naturally' inhibited against committing crimes because they have adverse consequences for others, since conventional and respected activities (such as private entrepreneurship) often manifest identical qualities:

> The ideal pecuniary man is like the ideal delinquent in his unscrupulous conversion of goods and persons to his own ends, and in a callous disregard for the feelings and wishes of others and of the remoter effects of his actions.

All these examples perhaps help to suggest that at least sometimes, and in some contexts, we are capable of a wide range of crimes. This is all that is required by postclassical criminology. The fact that most of us, most of the time, do not translate these capabilities into action is precisely what is seen as needing an explanation. The assumption is that it is relatively more fruitful to regard our conformity, rather than our criminality, as problematic.

Perhaps this position can best be tested by taking an extreme example – a crime which it would seem to be impossible to accept as being within the 'normal' range of human motivations: sexual abuse of children. Surely these crimes are accounted for by the existence of 'special' motives? And surely they are best explained in terms of how these special motives come about? The answer here could be simply to acknowledge this particular crime as an exception. After all, the postclassical position recognises that variability in human criminal motivations plays a part in accounting for the prevalence of crimes: it would not be too damaging to the overall position to allow that in *some* cases it plays the major part (provided that the exceptions only constitute a tiny proportion of total crime – which would certainly be the case with sexual abuse of children).

However, I am not sure that even in this case an exception must automatically be made. The advantages of the postclassical approach apply wherever the *motivations* towards particular criminal actions are vastly more prevalent than the *actions*. In all such cases the prevalence of such actions and the possibilities for their control are better accounted for by addressing the question of what it is that usually inhibits the actions, rather than by accounting for how the motivations arise. Unfortunately, the empirical evidence is not available to decide whether this applies to the case of sexual abuse of children. Currently, the evidence is suggesting that *both* the motives and the actions are more prevalent than was previously supposed. However, this does suggest that the motives are not so 'special' as to preclude the possibility of a considerable disparity between the prevalence of motives and the prevalance of actions. Whether this is the case or not, even the more special crimes such as this one cannot automatically be assumed to be outside the scope of the postclassical perspective.

Crime

So far I have discussed the different criminologies of the previous two centuries with little reference to the problem of the concept of 'crime' itself. Worse, I have sometimes used 'crime' and 'deviance' interchangeably – though I hope I have only done this where the argument has happened to apply equally to both. But clearly, some discussion of the subject-matter of postclassical criminology is in order.

First, it must be asserted that the subject-matter *is* crime, and not the more nebulous category of deviance. Second, crime is accepted to be a *legal* category – no attempt is being made to propose, as we saw some positivists tried to do, that we can arrive at some more objective conception that stands above the acts of human deliberation that constitute the process of legal definition. Crimes are violations of legal rules; legal rules are those rules that are defined and enforced by agencies of the state that have, ultimately, the authority to use coercion. Crimes thus come about through human beings interpreting and applying rules (which are themselves the product of human deliberation) to the actions of others. This is why it is extremely dangerous to imagine, as many positivist criminologists seemed to do, that such actions can be understood and explained without reference to these processes of definition and application. As we saw when considering the interactionist critique of positivism, there are two particularly important reasons for this: first, the processes of definition and application produce the data specifying the nature of, and the trends in, crime, and the characteristics of criminals that are subsequently used by criminologists to construct their theories and explanations; second, these processes of definition and application have consequences for the meanings, implications and justifications that those 'labelled' by them give to their own actions. Postclassical criminology must be alive to both of these considerations.

Fortunately, the legal definition of crime incorporates the assumption of its 'naturalness' to free and rational human beings, which was discussed in the previous section. Indeed, if the actions are not deemed to be free and rational (in the sense that the offenders are capable of understanding their nature, moral meaning and consequences) then they will not usually be defined as crimes in legal terms. Also, the fact that free, rational human beings are still seen as requiring organised discouragement from committing crime implies an acceptance of its 'naturalness'. This, incidentally, could help with the problem encountered earlier of incorporating unusual crimes such as child abuse in the postclassical perspective. If such crimes really are *entirely* accounted for by the possession of abnormal motives propelling their possessors into crime regardless of any other considerations, then it does not really possess the features that usually class actions as 'crimes'; rather, it would belong in some alternative category, such as mental illness.

As in the legal definition, the interactionist conception of crime also implicitly portrays it as something that ordinary people are likely to want to do. Crime is seen as *only* identifiable by the *discouraging* response it evokes. In other words, its sole defining feature (discouraging reaction) is predicated on the prior existence of the desire to do it. This applies regardless of the *content* of criminal defnitions which, for interactionists, are highly variable. Thus, between them, the legal and interactionist conceptions illustrate the point that crime, however relativistically it is viewed, always incorporates the assumption of the naturalness of human motivation towards it.

Postclassical criminology embraces the relativity of criminal definitions – though without necessarily accepting that they are, or have been, as randomly selective as interactionism sometimes seemed to suggest. But this poses a problem: if 'crimes' are diverse, changeable and selective, how can we expect to be able to make any *general* statements about the conditions that influence their prevalence? The answer, I think, involves a partial refutation of the interactionist position: crimes *do* share an intrinsic quality – they involve the knowing transgression of rules laid down and enforced by the state. And they involve actions that most people, at least sometimes, are likely to want to perform. It *is* perfectly conceivable that we can make some general statements about the conditions that influence our self-indulgence or self-restraint in relation to rules laid down and enforced by the state, particularly when the nature of those rules and the way they are enforced are included for consideration.

5 Sources of Control

By rejecting the stance of positivist criminology and by taking criminal motivations as given, postclassical criminology shifts the question from what causes crime to what influences people in the direction of conformity. The answer is in terms of incentives and disincentives. Any attempt to specify these incentives and disincentives would seem to get us back to something very much like the attempt to specify all possible human pleasures and pains which, as was mentioned in Chapter 1, was one of Bentham's less successful utilitarian ventures. Nevertheless, if we are to define what it is that influences our decisions whether or not to indulge our motivations towards crime we inevitably make suppositions about human needs or requirements, which are in turn predicated on assumptions about what it is that gives us pleasure or pain.

Throughout history moral philosophers, jurisprudentialists, anthropologists and sociologists (in their quests for universal moral ideals, natural law, cultural universals or minimum requirements for social life) have all, of necessity, been led into speculation about basic human needs as foundation stones for their theories. Most notable of the more recent examples would perhaps be Rawls (1972) with his assumption of 'primary goods' such as liberty, opportunity, wealth and self-respect, and Finnis (1980, p. 59) with his 'forms of good . . . that are irreducibly basic' of life, knowledge, play and aesthetic experience. At a rather more humble level of philosophical sophistication, sociologists of crime and deviance have built their theories on similar suppositions. Thrasher (1927), whom we encountered in Chapter 3 as one of the founders of a control perspective, borrowed Thomas's (1923) speculations as the basis of his universal childhood needs of security, response, recognition and desire for new experiences.

For the purposes of the postclassical perspective being developed here, Thrasher and Thomas highlight an important feature of these needs: they are as readily (often more readily) satisfied by deviant activity as they are by conventional. Thomas (1923, p. 38) nicely overstates this point in relation to his postulated needs (or 'wishes' as he calls them):

The moral good or evil of a wish depends on the social meaning or value of the activity which results from it. Thus the vagabond, the adventurer, the spendthrift, the bohemian are dominated by the desire for new experience, but so are the inventor and scientist; adventurers with women and the tendency to domesticity are both expressions of the desire for response; vain ostentation and creative artistic work both are designed to provoke recognition; avarice and business enterprise are actuated by the desire for security.

This point once again reinforces the assumption of the 'naturalness' of deviant motivations that underpins both the classical and the postclassical perspectives.

In these attempts to specify human needs two problems dominate: validating the particular 'needs' that are specified, and establishing their universality. These problems also obviously apply to the attempt about to be made here. As far as validation is concerned, there does not seem to be a lot to live up to. Most writers, including those mentioned above, invariably refer, in the last resort, to 'self-evidence' to 'rational' human beings as their authority. In the case of 'universality', whatever the authority ('cross-cultural studies' are popular) the claim tends to be belied by the fact that different writers have arrived at rather different (though by no means completely different) lists.

In the needs that I am proposing there is no claim to their universality over time and place, only that they are broadly applicable to most contemporary Western societies (more or less). My authority is that they are recognised and utilised by informal and formal agencies such as parents, schools, governments and criminal justice systems as 'sources' of control. I will be dealing with seven (although another claim I am not making is that of exhaustiveness): *affection, status, stimulation, autonomy, security, money* and *belief.*

These 'needs' constitute sources of control because they provide for both incentives and disincentives: their satisfaction can be used to lure us into conformity, and the threat of their denial can be used to divert us from criminality. The satisfaction provided by conformity is in competition with the often more immediate satisfaction that can be provided by crime. Consequently, agencies of control always operate by threatening to withdraw or actually withdrawing the satisfaction of these needs, in an attempt to redress the balance.

It must be stressed that the necessary level of fulfilment to encourage conformity is *relative*, not *absolute*. It is relative to what we perceive as being possible, through our knowledge of the experience of others, or from our own experiences in different periods of our lives. It is also, of course, relative to the nature and certainty of the losses we anticipate from indulging our deviant motivations. Both of these sets of expectations are variable, over different time-periods and in the different social settings in which we find ourselves. The social settings can sometimes change quite rapidly – as in the case of the urban riot – giving rise to sudden and dramatic changes in behaviour. Such variability of criminal behaviour has been difficult to explain in positivist theories which see criminality as resulting from specific, more or less permanent characteristics of particular 'types' of individual. A virtue of the postclassical perspective is that, although it too is concerned with differences in individual dispositions towards crime, it allows more readily for changes in such dispositions, and for a more dynamic relationship between them and the situations in which they are likely to be activated.

The complicated picture that emerges from this variability in the relative expectations that we have of reward or loss from criminal as against conforming behaviour is compounded by the fact that our different needs and requirements may often pull in quite different directions. An obvious example is the contradiction that may arise between the requirements for parental affection, on the one hand, and status with peers, on the other. On other occasions, however, they may reinforce each other. In the ensuing chapters I will be looking at these processes in more detail. But first, I will say a little more about what actually constitutes these needs and requirements and how they operate as sources of control.

Affection

Our need for ties of mutual affection – our desire to please, and our fear of hurting, or losing the affection, of those we care about – provides the earliest and one of the most potent sources of control of our deviant motivations. Later, the presence, or even the existence, of the people we care about may not be necessary for their influence to apply, for we may retain the desire to be the kind of person who would have won their affection and approval. But the loss or gradual erosion of ties of affection is nevertheless a liberator of our criminality; never to have experienced them is perhaps the greatest liberator of all. Most criminological theories have, in various ways, acknowledged their significance. Usually, they have been recognised in the context of our early years in the family, since this is their dominant source during a period of particular dependence, and because later childhood is the age at which officially recorded criminality is at its greatest. Consequently, this particular instrument of control will loom large when we consider the family later.

It is clearly the case, however, that although the lack of ties of affection liberates criminal tendencies, their existence does not *necessarily* guarantee conformity. A vital additional factor is required: that those we are tied to disapprove of criminal acts (as they are defined) and that our own criminal acts would risk hurting them, or the diminution of their affection. The significance of affection is thus dependent on a pre-existing degree of acceptance of conformity; there must be a shortage of 'parental Fagins' as Matza (1964) put it. If subcultures exist where there is a lack of acceptance, or where the prohibitions of 'crimes' are not applied to victims seen as 'outsiders', then affective ties will be irrelevant to the control of crime. Thus, despite their apparent primacy and the universal significance given to them in criminological research, they are themselves dependent on the pre-existence and effective operation of other controls.

Status

Like affection, status relates to our feelings about other peoples' feelings for us. But it is different in nature. It is less intimate and based on different emotions. It relates to feelings of respect, admiration, importance, sometimes even fear, that we wish to evoke in others. Though such feelings are usually also involved in our intimate, affectionate relationships, they are not absolutely necessary to them. Status relates to our concern for our standing in the eyes of people more distant from us. Where affection is the preserve of family and friends, status is more the preserve of the wider peer group or community.

We also need status in our own eyes, as well as in the eyes of others; status, as I wish to use it here, includes self-esteem as well as reputation. These two elements tend, of course, to go together; but they are not synonymous. It is difficult, but not impossible to have self-esteem without reputation; easier, perhaps, to have reputation without self-esteem.

The negative side of reputation is stigma. Fear of the loss of reputation, or the acquisition of an unfavourable one in the form of stigma, can act as an important constraint. These fears may be greater, for example, than those which we attach to the actual penalties imposed by the law – hence the use, and fear, of publicity in relation to criminal offences. But the caveat that was applied to affection applies even more strongly to status: it only acts as a constraint in settings where criminal activity is generally unfavourably evaluated. Indeed, in this respect status is a less reliable control than affection, since it is usually available in more varied forms. Status is about 'being somebody' and not necessarily about being liked. And to be feared is to be somebody.

The varied forms in which status is available have been recognised by social controllers, and have made them wary of too much reliance on stigmatisation: conventional stigma can provide deviant status. Penal reformers, especially those concerned with children, have consequently argued for playing it down, and penal legislation (again, mostly in relation to children) has sometimes responded.

It was mentioned earlier that the requirements for status and for affection may pull in quite different directions. There is often a kind of tension between them: the stances for some forms of status (for example, for masculinity) may act as barriers to affection. And real affection may negate such stances. Such tensions may be particularly significant in the adolescent peer group.

Stimulation

As was noted earlier, Thrasher (1927), borrowing from Thomas (1923), rated the 'desire for new experiences' as one of his universal childhood need. I have in mind something similar under the heading of 'stimulation'. It refers to our need for physical and emotional experience – excitement, danger, relaxation, challenge (physical or intellectual), humour, sex, art, music. Individual constellations of these requirements are infinitely varied, of course. Some of them, sometimes, can be at least partially satisfied vicariously rather than directly (when we are audiences or spectators). They can also, of course, be satisfied by crime (again, vicariously as well as actually).

The need for stimulation has been recognised and utilised by social controllers at all levels, throughout history. Being sent to your room by your parents, being kept in after school, being given mindless repetitive tasks to do – are all deliberate withdrawals of stimulation. Treats and incentives invariably take the form of opportunities for stimulation. In the penal sphere, the final, and total withdrawal of stimulation – in the form of solitary confinement – has been one of the most ubiquitous forms of punishment.

Autonomy

The significance of autonomy is perhaps best illustrated by considering its absence. Matza (1964, p. 188) described among his delinquents a 'mood of fatalism', 'the experience of seeing one's self as effect. It is elicited by being "pushed around" and yields the feeling that one's self exercises no control over the circumstances surrounding it and the destiny awaiting it.' The denial of autonomy – in the form of imprisonment – is also one of the principle weapons used in the formal penal apparatus to attempt to control crime. But as Matza's quotation makes clear, its absence can be felt regardless of any formal attempt to withdraw it.

Since crimes usually involve positive, self-expressive acts, they are ideally suited to the task of asserting our autonomy. They 'make something happen'. Because, by our definition, crimes are things that most people, on some occasions, will want to do, their constraint is a constraint of our autonomy. Our compliance will consequently depend to some extent on the opportunities for self-expression through conventional avenues. If they are absent, then we will feel freer to deviate.

Our 'need' for autonomy is not, of course, total and universal, any more than any of the needs and requirements under discussion here. Indeed it illustrates the probabilistic nature of these arguments rather well. The significance of autonomy (or rather the threat of its loss) in relation to crime control is generally recognised because of its association with imprisonment. Yet we clearly do not always require it. Sometimes some people wish to withdraw into settings deliberately chosen for their regulation and predictability, such as the armed forces, nunneries, monasteries – even prison itself. But such cases are exceptions, sometimes perhaps simply reflecting the relative lack of satisfaction of needs on the outside (especially in the case of the 'choice' of prison). Generally, our need for autonomy, and the fear of its loss, are important factors in influencing our decisions about criminal actions.

Security

Security refers to our need to feel free of the actual experience of, or threat of, physical discomfort or injury. In a sense, it is the counterpart of our need for autonomy: while autonomy is the freedom to make things happen, security is the freedom from things we do not want to happen.

If the conventional realms of activity are not accompanied by a sense of security then we will feel less committed to them – we will be more likely to 'take the law into our own hands'; insecurity is associated with lawlessness. Conversely, if we anticipate the loss of security through our own lawlessness, we will be that much more likely to conform.

Historically, threatening our security in this 'physical' sense has been the most common way in which penal systems have attempted to force our compliance (through capital and corporal punishments). They have usually relied on the grossness of the physical threat, rather than its certainty, to do the work. In recent times, however, physical threats have been dropped in favour of threats to our autonomy and money. But this has only been at the 'official' level; as Sykes (1958) and many subsequent studies have shown, loss of a sense of physical security is still one of the major 'pains of imprisonment' as perceived by inmates.

Money

It almost goes without saying that in contemporary society a certain amount of money is an important human requirement, not necessarily for its own sake (though that may also be the case), but because it is the wherewithal for other requirements. To claim money as a major human goal is not to make any specific claim about 'human nature' (such as its mercenariness) since it is not so much a goal in itself but the facilitator of almost all possible human goals – expressive, artistic, acquisitive or whatever. Again, this is not to claim that we all aspire to it equally: it is simply to claim that, whatever our personal specific goals, *some* amount of money is almost invariably required for their realisation. The criminal justice system, of course, now recognises this even more than it recognises our need for autonomy: monetary penalties are by far the most common form of penalty that it uses in its attempt to control crime.

To claim money as a current human necessity, however, is not to claim the concomitant necessity of any particular mode for its generation and distribution (such as the capitalist economy). Nor is it to deny that a society capable of providing for the fulfilment of all human needs, all the time, would eliminate the need for money altogether. Unfortunately, at the moment there are no known examples of the latter being achieved, and there is no way of knowing whether it is achievable. So for the time being it would be prudent to treat money as a major variable in our relationship with crime and conformity.

Belief

We are more likely to conform if we believe in the rules and constraints that conformity imposes upon us. Although belief is not a 'need' in the same sense as the others, its strength is dependent on the satisfaction of a need, as we will see. It is also similarly a source of control; its satisfaction or neglect will affect the likelihood of our compliance.

Belief does not guarantee anything, of course. We are perfectly capable of breaking rules we believe in (for, example, where conformity fails adequately to satisfy our other needs) and we may comply in the absence of belief (where the fear of the consequences of non-compliance is strong). As with all the needs and requirements that constitute the sources of control, its influence is mediated by the influence of the others.

A question that arises is whether belief exercises any independent influence at all. It could be that it is reducible to the other needs; that our belief in convention is purely a function of the degree to which it satisfies our needs for affection, status, and so on. Clearly, it must be acknowledged that this is likely to be the case. But I think we can allow belief some independent influence as well, and the basis of that independence can be derived from the classical conception of our self-interested rationality. This, it will be remembered, enables us to perceive the deferred, but ultimate greater, advantages of self-denial: we will accept the immediate constraints of convention if they are seen as serving some general advantage. Belief, in this sense, facilitates a more abstract acceptance of conformity; it leads us to conform in the absence of *immediate* personal advantage from doing so (or even where it would be to our advantage not to do so).

The offer of some greater good in the future, however, is not usually sufficient to guarantee our belief in present conformity, and it is in this connection that we must introduce an additional need: the need for a sense of fairness, or justice. That is, we must also feel that the immediate personal sacrifices that are expected of us are just and fair, if we are to comply. To feel this we need to be sure that other people are making similar sacrifices or, if they are not, that there are acceptable grounds for their not doing so. We must feel that the existing social arrangements allow for equal, or justifiably unequal, satisfaction of our other needs, if we are to believe in conformity. In the legal context, we need to feel that the prohibitions of laws, in the way they are defined and in the way they are applied, are justifiable and influence us all equally (or, again, if they do not, that they discriminate on acceptable grounds). The strength of our belief in conformity, based on this 'sense of justice' may act quite independently of considerations of immediate personal advantage.

Sources and Contexts of Control

The sources of control play their part to varying degrees and in varying combinations in the different contexts that constitute our social worlds. In the following three chapters I will be examining their significance in three broad contexts: *family and community; the social divisions brought about by age, class, race and gender*; and *the criminal justice system and crime control policy*. In doing so I will be making frequent reference to the empirical research findings of criminologists working mostly in the positivist tradition. Given the difficulties involved in this kind of work, especially when it is based on 'official' data (see Chapter 3), this may seem rather dubious. In particular, there is almost always the problem of determining whether the 'findings' are findings about crime and criminals, or about the assumptions, beliefs and stereotypes of those who 'label' people as criminals. Unless some attempt is made to address such problems it is unreasonable to suppose that such findings have any privileged status over any other kinds of assertion.

However, where comparisons can be made with alternative sources of data, and where it is possible to provide some evidence to counter the possibility that the findings are due purely to 'data collection' effects, we can perhaps arrive at some tentative conclusions. In the following chapters I will attempt to do this, wherever possible. But even then, this is not to suggest, in the way that the positivists often seemed to do, that the result is some form of objective, scientific exercise.

Also, the associations that will be discussed, and the interpretations of them in postclassical terms that will be offered, should not be seen as suggesting the operation of 'causes' or 'determinants', even where such language has been used by those involved in establishing the associations. The earlier discussion should have made clear that the postclassical perspective does not allow for the degree of certainty or inevitability that such terms are usually taken to imply. Rather, they should be seen as establishing 'influences' pulling in particular directions (in contexts where, for particular individuals, there are many other influences), sometimes supportive, sometimes contradictory, but always open to some degree of individually idiosyncratic interpretation.

6 Contexts of Control, I:
Family and Community

Since officially measured crime is most prevalent among the young, and since the majority of adult criminals started out as youthful delinquents, much criminological research has concentrated on the immediate social environment in which delinquents grow up – family relationships, peer relationships, school and area of residence. Needless to say, however, these relationships are themselves located in a wider social and economic context. The implications of this wider context for the more immediate social environment have been one of the more divisive issues in criminological theorising. Some (usually psychologists) have given primacy to family relationships and concentrated almost exclusively on them. Others (usually sociologists) have taken wider, social class divisions as primary, and treated family, peer, school and neighbourhood factors as being expressions of these divisions. To be comprehensive, the postclassical perspective must make sense of things at all these levels, as well as the relationship between them. In this chapter I will be starting 'at the bottom', so to speak, with the family and then working out into the wider social settings. The special problems of the way in which these settings are influenced by divisions of class, race and gender will be dealt with in the next chapter.

Family

> Although denied in some theories and ignored in others, the fact that delinquents are less likely than non-delinquents to be closely tied to their parents is one of the best documented findings of delinquency research (Hirschi, 1969, p. 85).

After some false starts, resulting mostly from early attempts to associate delinquency with oversimplified measures of family breakdown such as the broken home and maternal separation (Bowlby, 1946), subsequent studies focusing on the *quality* of family relationships have clearly established the link between delinquency and low levels of supervision, affectional ties, harmony and intimacy of communication with parents. In the United States, for example, this was confirmed by

Rodman and Grams (1967) in their detailed survey of family studies for the 1967 President's Commission on Law Enforcement and Administration of Justice. In Britain, West (1969) and West and Farrington (1973) have perhaps provided the most detailed confirmation of such findings, reinforced by the wide-ranging survey of Rutter and Giller (1983, Chapter 6). Nye (1958) and Hirschi (1969) have provided the evidence most directly relevant to the postclassical perspective in their data showing that delinquents are less 'attached' to their parents (identify with them, care about them, and communicate with them less). Hirschi's work was subsequently replicated and confirmed by Hindelang (1973).

Recently, following a series of studies, Wilson (1987) has argued that it is the degree of parental *supervision* that is crucial in controlling delinquency. Riley and Shaw (1985), however, have disputed this and a complex definitional and methodological dispute has ensued between them (see Wilson, 1987; Riley, 1987). However, Riley (1987, p. 422) makes the following salient point:

> As Hirschi put it 'the important consideration is whether the parent is psychologically present . . . children who perceive their parents as unaware of their whereabouts are highly likely to have committed delinquent acts'. Riley and Shaw showed that the crucial factor in understanding why some parents were able to exert closer control over their teenagers than others was the parent–child relationship itself. Teenagers who got on badly with their parents were less likely to be well supervised.

Consequently, regardless of this specific dispute, it seems reasonable to conclude from the evidence both that supervision is less likely to be effective without close ties between parent and child, and that close ties are not likely to be effective unless they are actually utilised for purposes of supervision.

The point has been made several times that findings such as those cited above, when based on official data, should be treated with great caution. They are always open to the alternative interpretation that they simply reflect the tendency of agents of social control to define children from such home backgrounds as officially delinquent. However, in this case such arguments are more difficult to sustain. In those studies (for example, Hirschi's) that have used self-report data, the findings have mostly held just as strongly. Whatever the limitations of these alternative data (and there are, of course, many) they are not subject to this particular form of bias. Combined with the official data, the overall picture is probably as convincing as it is feasible to be in this area.

In terms of the sources of control specified earlier, these findings clearly relate to the importance of primary affectional ties and, in some instances, to the need for security. Some control theorists, such as Briar and Piliavin (1965), see fear of losing the affection and support of parents as one aspect of the personal 'stake' that people have in conformity. But this is perhaps a rather cynical view. There is, after all, more to affectional ties than a simple perception of personal advantage. They usually, though not always, involve feelings of empathy and concern which transcend such purely personal considerations. As I have stressed earlier, although postclassical criminology is rooted in the classical view of our natural selfishness, this is not to exclude all other, sometimes contradictory, qualities – such as empathy and concern. But either way, where such ties and feelings are absent, where the person concerned sees their family setting as providing little or nothing positive for them, this seems to be a very significant liberator of whatever natural proclivities towards actions defined as crimes that they may have.

In the earlier discussion of affectional ties as a source of control it was pointed out that although their absence is a primary factor in producing crime, their presence will only produce conformity where those to whom the person is attached are themselves conventional. The findings appear to suggest that, at least for Britain and the United States, this is predominantly the case: parents, overwhelmingly, are not supportive of their children's delinquency. That is why the presence of affectional ties is such an important controlling factor. It is worth speculating, however, as to whether this general finding may be masking significant subgroups where this is not the case. That is, is it possible that there are some subgroups where crime is not particularly frowned upon and where, consequently, affectional ties are not protective against crime? Interestingly, Hirschi's data provide an inkling that this may indeed sometimes be the case. In his study, children whose fathers had a history of unemployment or being on welfare were both particularly delinquent and equally attached to their fathers, whether delinquent or not. This suggests the possibility of particularly alienated sections of the community where there is a low general stake in conformity, high crime rates and thus a situation where affectional ties have no effect on criminal involvement. Hirschi himself dismissed this finding because it did not hold for the lower class as a whole. But it raises the question as to whether there may be more sharply defined alienated groups where special conditions apply in relation to crime. I will be returning to this point later when considering peer groups, neighbourhoods and social class generally.

In the postclassical perspective human beings are seen as dynamic and changing according to different circumstances, rather than locked into rigid personality types established in early childhood. Consequently, we should expect that changes in affectional ties will be related to criminal involvement in adulthood, as well as childhood and adolescence (although, of course, other factors associated with age may influence the *overall* level of involvement in crime of different age groups). Unfortunately, there is much less research evidence relating to adult criminals. However, what little there is – mainly relating to marital experience – does lend some further support to the significance of affectional ties.

Various studies, in the positivist tradition, have long shown that prisoners and habitual offenders have markedly higher rates of divorce and separation and marital disharmony (Morris, 1951; Hammond and Chayen, 1963; West, 1963; Morris and Morris, 1963). West's study also found that among the 'intermittent' recidivists (those who had gaps of four years or more without convictions) marriage or cohabitation often played an important part in their lives during their crime-free periods. However, Rutter and Giller (1983), in their survey of the evidence in this area, show that it suggests that marriage can also increase criminal involvement when the marriage is to a criminal spouse – once again illustrating this significant limitation of affectional ties.

However, more detailed studies of particular categories of adult offender have tended to support an association between isolation from or disruption of personal relationships and criminal involvement. A good example is Lemert's (1958) study of cheque forgers, where he provides a useful description of the effects of the breakdown of such ties (quoted by Box, 1971, pp. 142–3, in his analysis of the attachment bond in his version of control theory):

> a . . . discriminating factor was suggested by the unusually high rate of divorce and separation among married forgers and the high incidence of family alienation and repudiation among single forgers . . . The marital ruptures quite frequently were followed by continuous drunkenness, job inefficiency, occupational detachment and occupational mobility, often in decided contrast to the predivorce history.

The more biographical evidence of both West and Lemert counters, to some extent, the obvious criticism that it may be that the association between involvement in crime and social isolation is simply because crime leads to social isolation, rather than the other way round. On the other hand, the evidence certainly allows for the possibility that the consequences of criminal involvement can 'feed back' into social isolation (a point to which I will return later when considering labelling theory in relation to the criminal justice system).

Despite the generally supportive findings, it is undoubtedly the case that the relationship between lack of close affectional family ties and crime is less well established for adult crime than it is for youthful delinquency. And, once again, the important proviso applies: such ties must be to conventional figures if they are to influence in the direction of conformity.

School

The first setting, outside of the family, which offers the child conventional avenues for personal goal fulfilment is the school. Indeed, it both constitutes such avenues in the present, and is a key determinant of them in the future. However, it also requires considerable sacrifice of personal autonomy in the present. Because of this sacrifice we cannot assume, as the 'strain' perspective seemed to do, that there is even an initial commitment to the school on the part of the child. The postclassical perspective would lead us to expect that this commitment has to be won, in the face of fairly stiff competition from the immediate advantages of truancy. The fact that attendance at school is enforced by law is a formal recognition of this situation. The fact that the relationship between truancy, classroom disruption and poor academic performance and other forms of delinquency is one of those relatively rare universal findings of criminological research (European Committee on Crime Problems, 1972: Rutter and Giller, 1983) is further evidence that the school has a problematic status in relation to crime and convention.

Yet, despite these findings, the school has received relatively little criminological attention compared, for example, with family and peer-group relationships. This has been because most of the studies have suggested that the school failures associated with delinquency are themselves the result of prior, predisposing factors in the individual make-up or family experience of the children coming into the schools. That is, although different schools have very different delinquency rates, this is usually accounted for by differences in their intakes rather than by differences in what happens in the different schools (Farrington, 1972; Rutter *et al.*, 1979).

One 'personal' characteristic that has been found to relate strongly to both delinquency and school failure is academic ability, as measured by various forms of IQ test (West and Farrington, 1973; Hirschi and Hindelang, 1977). Even if we were to deny that this characteristic is 'personal' in the sense of being inherited, this finding seems damaging to the postclassical perspective, which eschews any personal characteristics as explanations of delinquency. The point is, however, that even if ability *were* inherited, it would not, in itself, provide us with an explanation of delinquency, nor would it be incompatible with an explanation in terms of individual experience (a point that was made in the discussion of inheritance and crime in Chapter 2). Consider the following explanation, for example: children of low measured ability (however contentiously defined, and however determined) are treated as inferior by others; as a result they have less at stake in terms of conventional relationships and reputation; this in turn means they have less to lose in indulging whatever delinquent proclivities they have (and they do have, like everyone else). We might expect this to apply particularly to the school, which specially emphasises academic ability. The school would offer such children nothing either in terms of present reward, or promises of future rewards. Their rejection of it would be perfectly rational.

This explanation is entirely compatible with the postclassical perspective. However, it does also suggest that different schools *would* have different effects, since it would be reasonable to suppose that some would be worse than others at promoting a sense of self-esteem and worthwhileness among their pupils (even to the extent of, in some cases, failing to instil it in those who *do* have ability). There is, in fact, some evidence to support this. Despite the tendency for school effects to be explained away by other factors, this has not been entirely the case (Rutter *et al.*, 1979; Finlayson and Loughran, 1976; Graham, 1986). And the differences that have been found are compatible with the suggestion that it is the pupils' perceptions of the worthwhileness of their school experience that are crucial. Finlayson and Loughran, for example found considerable differences in the general atmosphere between different schools that could not be accounted for by differences in intake. The high-delinquency schools were characterised by inflexibility of social control and low sense of involvement and personal satisfaction among the pupils. Similarly, in his assessment, Graham concludes that variations in schools' success in providing pupils with a sense of achievement and self-esteem was related to their likelihood of becoming involved in delinquency.

In an earlier, non-comparative, study Hargreaves (1967) suggested that within the school that he studied the combination of rigid streaming by ability and lack of rewards for lower-stream pupils led to a subculture among the latter where opposition to the school and its objectives conferred status, and where delinquency was particularly prevalent. The evidence from Hargreaves's participant observation approach showed how this negative response to the school made sense from the point of view of the pupils defined as being of low ability. Whatever the origins of their low ability, it was the *response* it evoked from the school that *explained* the negativism.

Finally, a more recent American study (Wiatrowski, Griswold and Roberts, 1981) concerned with testing control theory, concluded that the school was as important as the family in developing children's 'bonds' to conformity. They explain this by the conventional sociological argument that in modern complex societies schools have taken over the former family functions of socialising children (or 'bonding them to convention', in control theory terms).

Of course, a simpler alternative explanation of the association between poor school performance, truancy and delinquency could be that pupils who are troublesome to schools are more likely to be *defined* as delinquent. That is, that troublesome pupils are not in fact more delinquent, it is just that their delinquency is more likely to be officially recorded. This is complicated by the fact that truancy is usually defined as being a form of delinquency; but it could be that this means that other forms of delinquency that truants are involved in may be more likely to be recorded. Certainly, the school does act as an important referral agency for recording delinquents (Bottomley and Coleman, 1981). Graham (1986) notes that there is evidence to suggest that magistrates appear to be particularly influenced by the contents of the school report and reference to school matters in social enquiry reports (though this only suggests the possibility that school matters influence the issuing of care orders, not that they determine pupils' chances of being defined as delinquent). But anyway, there is a chicken-egg argument here: it could be that schools are more likely to refer the delinquency of troublesome pupils because they know that such pupils *are* more involved in delinquency. The only alternative evidence that we have is, once again, from self-report studies. These have tended to find that the association between delinquency and the school factors holds just as strongly for self-reported delinquents as for official ones (Hirschi and Hindelang, 1977).

Peers

The tendency for delinquents to consort with other delinquents is another virtually universal finding of traditional criminological research. The problem is, however, what to make of this finding. It is a finding that is most specifically associated with learning theories – indeed, they seemed to rely on little else. But, as we saw in Chapter 2, quite apart from the often nebulous and all-encompassing nature of the concept of 'learning', such theories failed to account for how delinquent associates came to be around in the first place; somebody must have 'invented' delinquency originally, in which case, why could not the others, or all, have done so?

For the postclassical perspective there is, of course, no problem of invention. Delinquency does not have to be invented: it is already there as a potentiality. Consequently, the postclassical view tends to favour a 'birds of a feather' explanation of the association of delinquents rather than a learning theory: delinquents tend to *choose* delinquent associates because they neither attract, nor are attracted by, conventional peers. Thus the association is only of secondary significance; it results from the attraction of likeness of those already dissociated from convention. But this is not to detract from its importance as a support for delinquent activity. The association of delinquents provides attachments, reputation, self-esteem and security for those not receiving much of these things from convention. They are not, of course, 'driven' into it by frustration; they simply choose it because it is the better option.

The above analysis, however, includes several assumptions that require some further exploration. One important one is that delinquents are recruited rather than created. Box (1981), in his analysis of this question from his 'control' perspective points out that it implies two propositions: first, that conventional adolescents are less likely to associate with delinquent peers 'because they are too sensitive to the views of their parents or teachers, or because they fear to risk their reputation or because they believe delinquency would be wrong'; second, that where conventional adolescents *do* acquire delinquent friends, they are less likely to commit delinquent acts than their delinquent associates. Box cites various empirical studies in support of these propositions, and quotes Hirschi's (1969, p. 159) conclusion:

> contrary to subculture theorists and 'countless mothers', the gang only rarely recruits 'good' boys, when it does manage to recruit them, only rarely induces them to commit delinquent acts . . . the evidence strongly supports the view that the boy's stake in conformity affects his choice of friends rather than the other way round.

The postclassical perspective allows for the possibility that delinquent groups exist that are, directly or indirectly, *supportive* of delinquency. That is, the shortage of 'parental Fagins', mentioned earlier, is not matched by an equivalent shortage of Artful Dodgers (although their influence is not usually upon innocent Olivers – to wring the last drop out of the metaphor!). To suggest that such groups are supportive of and therefore reinforce delinquency is to imply that they are characterised by meaningful relationships – that the members care about other members' opinions of them. In other words, we would expect that, unlike attachments with parents, attachments with peers would be just as strong for delinquents as for non-delinquents.

Hirschi's study found this not to be the case; he found his delinquents to be significantly less attached to their peers when compared with non-delinquents. He concluded that it seemed to be a general principle that attachments, where they occur, are invariably associated with conformity. This finding was something of a surprise, even to Hirschi. It was also a finding that has found least support elsewhere. Hindelang (1973), for example, in his replication of Hirschi's work, confirmed every finding except this one. He found his delinquents to be equally attached to their peers. Conger (1976), using similar measures to Hirschi, also failed to confirm it. Further, Hirschi (1969, p. 157) himself acknowledged that his own data showed that 'there is an effect of delinquent gang membership much beyond that suggested by the "birds of a feather proverb"'. In the light of all the evidence it seems reasonable to conclude that delinquents' attachments to their peers, though possibly less strong than for non-delinquents, are still strong enough to have some reinforcing effect on their delinquent behaviour.

There is an additional important implication of these findings: they suggest that groups of delinquents share values and beliefs that are at least permissive of delinquency (if they are to have any reinforcing effect). I say 'permissive' since the postclassical perspective would not require *positive* reinforcement; insulation from outside negative response would be adequate to enhance their feeling of freedom to express their delinquent motivations, which the postclassical perspective takes for granted. This allows for Matza's point, dealt with in Chapter 2, that delinquents in fact tend to be predominantly conventional rather than actually pro-delinquent in their beliefs. As we saw, other evidence suggested that they nevertheless tend to be significantly less supportive of conventional values than non-delinquents. And Matza himself showed how delinquents share 'techniques of neutralisation' (Matza and Sykes, 1957) which enable them to justify their delinquent actions 'in the circumstances' and at least temporarily neutralise whatever commitments to convention they have. Quite apart from that, as we saw earlier in this chapter, Matza has also drawn attention to the similarity between delinquent and conventional values at the 'subterranean' level. Many subsequent studies of various more or less deviant youth subcultures have emphasised the way in which their deviant activities express the same kinds of need for status, recognition and stimulation as do conventional activities (see Brake, 1980). All these findings suggest that delinquent groups share a sufficiently permissive view of delinquency to reinforce the delinquent proclivities that they bring into the group.

These conclusions do not alter the fact that, despite the high profile that delinquent groups and subcultures have had in criminological research, their influence on delinquent activity is secondary. Their effect is predicated on the prior existence of individuals already freed from strong commitments to convention.

Neighbourhood

The Chicago school of sociology, at its most productive in the inter-war years, was famous for its minutely detailed measurement and theoretical explanation of what seemed to be the most striking and universal social characteristic of crime: its concentration in particular types of residential area. It established what was to become one of the taken-for-granted starting points for sociological theorising about crime: that it is much more likely to be found in the most socially and economically disadvantaged, physically deteriorated sectors of our towns and cities (see Shaw and McKay, 1942, for the Chicago findings). Later British evidence suggested that this finding held even when the most disadvantaged areas were not, in absolute terms, particularly physically deteriorated (big differences being found, for example, between initially physically similar Local Authority housing estates; see Baldwin and Bottoms, 1976; and Gill, 1977).

The Chicago findings were not quite universal. Some notable exceptions were found. Jewish and Chinese communities, for example, even when sharing the economic and physical conditions, did not necessarily share the same high crime rates (see Lander, 1954). Interestingly, it was their strong kinship ties that seemed to account for the difference, again illustrating the point (central to the postclassical perspective) that specific control factors (or their absence) are never decisive. They always operate in conjunction with, or in opposition to, a range of other factors.

Nevertheless, the relationship between high official crime rates and economically and physically disadvantaged areas of residence is sufficiently ubiquitous to warrant the amount of attention it has been given. More recent work has suggested that such findings cannot be accounted for by differences in policing, or the reporting or recording of crime in the different areas. Victim and self-report studies have generally upheld the differences (see Rutter and Giller, 1983, p. 203; and Bottoms and Mawby, 1987); and Baldwin (1974) and Mawby (1979) provide evidence to suggest that the high rates cannot be accounted for by special police initiatives. However, the question that arises is – what can we make of this relationship?

Two rather different explanations spring to mind. The first is that various forces (choice, or lack of it, economic considerations, housing authority policy) tend to congregate people who are already crime-prone, or who share personal circumstances associated with crime. The second is that such areas share general characteristics that are crime-productive – more than would be expected simply from the personal circumstances of the residents. A third possibility, of course, is that both these explanations apply.

There is certainly plenty of evidence to suggest that there are forces at work that tend to congregate those most economically disadvantaged. High-crime areas are invariably the least desirable (witnessed by the relatively large number of empty units) and lowest rent. The families that end up in them are consequently those with the lowest incomes and least power: unemployed, single-parent, and those with large numbers of children or high rates of physical and mental illness. There is also evidence to suggest that concentrating people with these problems in particular areas or estates is sometimes a result of deliberate housing policy (see for example Gill, 1977). And these family circumstances are themselves associated with high crime rates. Do the high rates, then, result simply from the summation of these personal circumstances, or is there some 'area effect' over and above that? Needless to say, it is extremely difficult to separate out such effects. However, Rutter and Giller (1983, p. 206), in their survey of the evidence, tentatively conclude that 'the social status of the area may be as important as (or more important than) the social status of the *individual*'.

In terms of the postclassical perspective, the picture that these findings tend to suggest is the following: the circumstances of individuals and families that are associated with a low stake in conformity (in terms of close and secure family ties, reputation and self-esteem, economic reward, and so on) also tend to lead them into being concentrated into the least desirable residential areas. The characteristics of such areas – poor and inappropriate housing conditions, poor schools and leisure facilities and, particularly significantly, stigmatisation for living in the area (see Armstrong and Wilson, 1973; and Gill, 1977) reduce the residents' stake in conformity still further. These are the settings where affectional ties, even where they are strong, are less likely to produce conformity (see the earlier findings in the discussion of the family). The net effect of the residential concentration is consequently to promote more crime than would otherwise have been the case.

A common misunderstanding of the Chicago 'criminal area' theory and its successors was that they constituted a kind of architectural explanation: that the criminogenic forces were seen as somehow built in to the bricks and mortar and physical layout of the area. The biological analogy sometimes used by the Chicago school (for example the idea of ecology) was perhaps to blame for this since it does imply biological organisms adapting to their physical surroundings. But this was not the intention; it was the *cultural* setting that these theorists were concerned with. More recently, however, architectural factors *have* become a focus of interest for criminologists. As we saw in Chapter 3 in the discussion of control theory, some recent control theorists have shifted attention to the crime-controlling potential of environmental design. The interest has been in the opportunities for self-surveillance, protection of property and generally increasing the risks of crime that can be physically built into the architecture and layout of residential areas. Needless to say, this is a rather different kind of problem from that discussed above and, as was explained earlier, is not the central focus of postclassical criminology.

Conclusion

Generally, criminological research findings on the relationship between family and community factors and crime seem to be in line with the expectations of the postclassical perspective. The risk of damaging close affectional ties (where the risk is present) is confirmed as an important influence against crime. To be defined as being of low ability at school is to be deprived of an important source of conventional reputation and self-esteem and means that education provides little in the way of either present personal rewards, or the future expectation of them. For those with already low stakes in convention, peer groups can provide supportive settings and a source of reputation and self-esteem for non-conventional, or less conventional, activities. Neighbourhoods can often be settings for the conglomeration and exacerbation of factors associated with a low stake in convention. As a background to these factors, which combine in varying, sometimes contradictory, constellations in individual cases, crime exists as an ever-present potentiality as an alternative source of money, autonomy, stimulation and status.

7 Contexts of Control, II: Social Divisions

In this chapter I will be looking at the 'context of control' in a rather different sense from that used in the discussion of family and community. Here I will be trying to assess the significance of underlying social divisions in terms of age, class, race and gender that differentiate people's opportunities, expectations and experiences. This is not entirely separate from the previous discussion, of course; at various points in Chapter 6 such divisions, especially in terms of class, were alluded to. But it remains to assess their significance more generally for the postclassical perspective.

The use of 'social' for categories such as age and race requires some comment, since they would normally be regarded as biological categories (I have used 'gender' rather than 'sex' specifically to avoid this implication). The reason for this designation is that, following the conclusions arrived at in Part One, postclassical criminology is concerned with the way in which membership of such categories influences *social experience*, rather than with any biologically determined crime-disposing characteristics that members may be supposed to possess.

Age

That crime is predominantly a phenomenon of adolescence is one of the most universal of criminological findings (see Hirschi and Gottfredson, 1983). That is, in all societies, officially recorded crime rates are low for children, peak at some point in adolescence, and decline fairly steadily from then on.

The reasons for these age differences have proved to be rather difficult to pin down. Most attempts have concentrated on age-correlates (such as family and school variables) to account for the variation. Yet Rowe and Tittle (1977) have shown that when all these correlates are controlled for, the age effect still remains. In fact, as Wilson and Herrnstein (1985, p. 145) conclude in their analysis, 'None of the correlates of age . . . explain crime as well as age itself'. The mainline sociological theories do not seem to have faired much better either. As Greenberg (1979) has pointed out, even those theories which concentrated on the apparently crime-prone adolescent group (such as the subcultural theories of Cohen and

Cloward and Ohlin), addressed themselves more to *within-age* group variation than to the age distribution itself.

As Wilson and Herrnstein note, it is not difficult to invent plausible-sounding explanations of the age distribution – and they do just that (1985, pp. 146–7) in terms of their own theoretical framework. Certainly, there would be no difficulty within the postclassical framework. Childhood, for example, is characterised by relative dependence on parents for need satisfaction, with consequently greater parental control and isolation from potential peer-support for deviant alternatives. For these reasons we might expect rates to be low (quite apart from the fact, of course, that legal definitions of crimes do not usually apply to the younger end of this age group). Adolescence, on the other hand, is a period of increasing independence of parents, greater availability of peer support and yet relative isolation from fully adult forms of need satisfaction; for these reasons we might expect rates to be high, and then decline as adult status is achieved.

Nevertheless, such explanations are highly speculative. In their somewhat nihilistic analysis, Hirschi and Gottfredson (1983) appeared to eliminate almost all theoretical perspectives as explanations of the age distribution of crime. Later, Hirschi (1986) draws a suggestive conclusion from his findings. Using his distinction between explanations of 'crime' (situational explanations of criminal events) and 'criminality' (explanations of criminal dispositions of offenders) he suggests that age, despite being an 'individual-level property', is a correlate of crime rather than of criminality. That is, it is a situational rather than an offender variable; it relates to crime through its significance for situational risks and opportunities rather than through its effects on individual dispositions to offend. As Hirschi points out, if this is the case, then age is of more particular interest to the situational, 'rational choice' branch of control theory than to his own.

The distinction made here by Hirschi, however, seems rather ambiguous. If, for example, the social experience of the adolescent age group is such as to make them *generally* more likely, as he puts it 'to discount the risk of injury from victims or guardians (or the risk of legal penalty)' (1986, p. 117), then this seems to constitute a *dispositional* rather than a purely situational factor. It seems as if Hirschi is only prepared to consider dispositions in terms of the way individuals evaluate the benefits of conformity, and not in terms of the way they evaluate the risks of non-conformity.

Whichever way this confusion is resolved, and despite the limitations of the evidence, it seems reasonable to conclude (albeit provisionally at this stage) that age differences in crime are explicable in terms of differences in the benefits of conformity and/or the risks of deviation that are contingent upon age, and are therefore compatible with the postclassical perspective.

Class

As we saw in Chapter 2, class divisions have been central to most sociological theories of crime. Their 'strain' assumption required the existence of forces pushing naturally conforming individuals into deviance, and virtually the only force specified was that of conventional ambitions thwarted by class barriers.

Fortunately, this almost exclusive dependence on class does not apply to the postclassical perspective. Here the failure to control individuals assumed to be naturally deviant can occur for a variety of reasons (such as the lack of affectional ties and the failure to cater for the needs of children defined as being of low ability, already dealt with in Chapter 6). Nevertheless, the postclassical perspective suggests that people disadvantaged in their access to conventional means of personal goal fulfilment would be more likely to turn to unconventional means, and class factors might be expected to be at least one source of such disadvantage. In other words, it would still seem to require at least *some* association between crime and low social class. Further, the wording I have just used is clearly reminiscent of anomie theory. Consequently, as promised in Chapter 2, the starting point is to propose an adjusted version of anomie theory divested of its 'strain' assumptions, compatible with the postclassical perspective and, with luck, not *entirely* dependent on class.

Anomie

First, let us look at what anomie theory seems to be saying in the most generalised terms: if people cannot achieve their goals via conventional means, then they will achieve them by unconventional ones. Keeping to this very general level, we may conceive of these goals as being the satisfaction of the kinds of personal need specified in Chapter 5. As was pointed out in that chapter, these are likely to include pecuniary goals simply because money is itself a very general goal (being the necessary means of achieving a wide range of personal satisfactions).

Stripped to its essentials in this way, 'anomie' can be separated from its anti-classical starting point. It includes no implication that human beings are 'naturally' conformist, but only that they share certain needs (in varying degrees and with varying priorities). There are conventional avenues for satisfying these needs, but there are other ways, too, and if the conventional ones are perceived as being unlikely to be fruitful, then they will be rejected in favour of the others. There is no 'push' required to make people overcome any 'natural' motivations towards the conventional avenues (because there is no such motivation).

The problem with the original anomie theory of Merton and the subcultural theorists was that they did not stop at this generalised specification. They assumed not only that people share *general* goal motivations, but that they also share the *conventional forms* of them. In Merton's formulation it was difficult in practice to distinguish the conventional goals from the conventional means: both seemed to boil down to success in the educational system and the achievement of a conventionally high-status, well-paid occupation. It was the assumption of the universality of these *specific*, middle-class orientations that made anomie a 'strain' theory. And, as we saw, it was this aspect of anomie that proved its downfall. It depended on delinquents being frustrated aspirants to conventional goal forms, with abnormally large 'gaps' between their conventional aspirations and expectations – a finding that eluded almost all research attempts.

The distinction between the postclassical and the traditional anomie images of the delinquent was neatly captured in a contemporary criticism of subcultural theory by Bordua (1961). He compared, unfavourably, the anomie-based interpretations of gang delinquency of Cohen and Cloward and Ohlin with the much earlier formulation by Thrasher (1927), whom we have already encountered (in Chapter 3) as an early exponent of a control-style perspective:

> I have purposely attempted to convey [Thrasher's] distinctive flavour of essentially healthy boys satisfying universal needs in a weakly controlled and highly seductive environment. Compared to the deprived and driven boys of more recent formulations with their status problems, blocked opportunities (or psychopathologies if one takes a more psychiatric view). Thrasher describes an age of innocence indeed . . . delinquency and crime were attractive, being a 'good boy' was dull. They were attractive because they were fun and were profitable and because one could be a hero in a fight. Fun, profit, glory and freedom is a combination hard to beat, particularly for the inadequate conventional institutions that formed the competition (Bordua, 1961, p. 123).

The postclassical image of anomie is not one which involves delinquents totally rejecting conventional values and replacing them with delinquent ones, as subcultural theory seemed to suggest. As we saw in Chapter 2, this degree of differentiation between delinquents and non-delinquents has always been difficult to establish. Rather, in the postclassical perspective, delinquents still adhere to conventional values but have significantly demoted them, leaving themselves freer to indulge their delinquent ones (as evidenced in the research findings cited in Chapter 2).

To recapitulate, the postclassical, 'strain-free' anomie theory says the following: *societies which provide conventional avenues for achieving personal goals which discriminate against certain sections of the community (for whatever reason) are unlikely to be very successful in committing those sections of the community to conventional lines of activity.* General as this is, it retains the idea of deregulation and erosion of conventional values which is central to the original conception of anomie. It also avoids any *specific* dependence on class: it can clearly incorporate other reasons why individuals or groups of individuals may be discriminated against in terms of access to conventional forms of personal goal fulfilment.

Nevertheless, there is still a clear implication in this adjusted version of anomie that economic and social disadvantage would be one systematic form of discrimination. Yet, despite the fact that it is usually found to be the case in the official criminal statistics, in more recent times the relationship between crime and low social class has come to be regarded with the deepest suspicion. Three lines of attack can be identified. First, at the individual level, alternative sources of data (such as self-report data) have failed to confirm the association (or have found a far less significant one). Second, substantial reductions in the absolute levels of poverty in most Western societies have almost invariably been associated with massive *increases* rather than *decreases* in crime rates. Third, official definitions of crime and their methods of enforcement are class-biased in a way that substantially underrecords higher–class 'crime'. Each of these allegations requires some attention.

Official and Self-report Data

Given that all the major sociological theories had more or less taken it for granted that crime was concentrated in the lower social class groups it was ironic, as well as shocking, that it should be this finding more than any other that failed to be confirmed by the self-report studies that came into fashion in the 1960s. However, the vast array of such studies now available have not been entirely consistent on this matter. So what kinds of conclusion, if any, can we draw from them (see Box, 1981, Chapter 3; and Rutter and Giller, 1983, Chapter 4 for useful surveys)?

First, self-report studies have always shown that the more trivial criminal offences are far more prevalent, among all social groups, than the official statistics would have us believe. This in itself could be seen as a problem for traditional theories – especially 'strain' theories which require something 'special' to push naturally conforming people into crime; there is obviously something conspicuously non-special about trivial criminal offences. This finding presents no problem, on the other hand, for the postclassical perspective: the prevalence is simply explained by the low risks involved – in terms of the low probability of detection and the minimal nature of both the formal and informal sanctions that they attract.

Second, there appears to be a difference between Britain and the United States. In the latter there seems to have been a trend towards a declining class differential, even in *official* data. In Britain, the official data usually show a substantial difference, the self-report data a much lesser one (but still a difference).

Third, the studies generally tend to show, in both Britain and the United States, that for *more serious* offences there *is* a marked difference in the rates for the different social class groups, though still less than that found in the official statistics. Box (1981) was less convinced of this than were Rutter and Giller (1983). However, in connection with this point, some of the methodological problems of self-report studies have an important bearing. Wilson and Herrnstein (1985) point out that self-report studies tend to underrepresent the most serious offenders, who are also the lowest in socio–economic status (although this underrepresentation probably accounts for the underestimation of race and gender differences, too). In most studies, for example, respondents are simply asked whether they have 'ever' committed particular offences, and 'recidivists' are usually respondents who admit to 'more than one'. As Wilson and Herrnstein (1985, p. 37) point out: 'Such a truncated set of responses obscures differences between persons who break the law once or twice (many males have done that) and those who break it twenty, thirty or fifty times per year.' Of perhaps even greater importance is the fact that those youths who are frequently involved in serious crime are much less likely to be incorporated in self-report studies. This is because most studies are carried out at, or through contact with, schools and therefore exclude habitual truants and school drop-outs – precisely the people most likely to be involved in frequent and more serious crime. For these and other reasons (see Wilson and Herrnstein, 1985), self-report studies always tend to lead to the underrepresentation of the characteristics of the most significant group of offenders.

Finally, and perhaps most important, if more direct measures of economic and social disadvantage such as low income, unemployment and dependence on welfare are used rather than the much 'blunter' divisions such as manual and non-manual occupations, more significant differences do tend to be found – even in the case of self-report data. We have already seen, for example, that Hirschi (1969) – one of the main sources of opposition to the class-correlation thesis – found much higher rates of delinquency for boys with fathers on welfare. And in Britain West and Farrington (1973) and Farrington (1979) found a strong association between delinquency and low family income.

It seems reasonable to draw the tentative conclusion that while there is some evidence of class bias in the official data, self-report data still suggest that crime and delinquency, particularly of a more serious nature, are more prevalent among the economically and socially disadvantaged (defined more specifically than in terms of broad 'class' divisions). This fits in with the residential area findings discussed in the last chapter, confirming the suggestion that there are some areas, characterised by the concentration of people with high levels of economic deprivation, where crime and delinquency are sufficiently prevalent to negate the usually crime-controlling effects of close affectional ties. It also supports the postclassical version of anomie: that extreme economic disadvantage is one (though only one) source of isolation from access to conventional forms of personal goal satisfaction and hence of 'liberation' of naturally deviant tendencies.

Crimes Rates and Poverty Rates

The second blow dealt to class-based criminological theories came at a different level of analysis: the relationship between *rates* and *trends* of broad measures of economic disadvantage (poverty, unemployment) and crime rates. For criminologists on the political right, the evidence was conclusive – the prosperity of the 1960s and the anti-poverty programmes, especially in the United States, had been accompanied by a massive *increase* in crime rates; for them the alleged relationship between crime and poverty, the basis of almost all prior sociological theorising about crime, was disproved (see Wilson, 1975).

Arguments about the unreliability of crime-trend data and of the largely cosmetic nature of anti-poverty programmes do not seem to have proved adequate to cope with this mass of counter-evidence. Indeed, criminologists on the left have also tended to accept that the weight of the evidence is against a simplistic relationship between crude measures of poverty and crime rates (see Lea and Young, 1984). That is, although the worst off tend to have higher crime rates (as we saw in the previous subsection), this masks the fact that there is no relationship between crime rates and the *degree* of poverty experienced by the poorest sections of different societies or ethnic communities. And, more importantly, altering the *absolute* level of poverty experienced by such groups does not seem to affect their crime rate.

The picture is rather different, however, if we move from *absolute* to *relative* economic indices. Box (1987), in his detailed analysis of the evidence on the relationship between various economic factors and crime in a range of industrialised countries, found that one particular index stood out, without exception, as being strongly related to criminal activity: the degree of income inequality (as measured by indices of income dispersion).

What are we to make of this? Lea and Young (1984) would be clear on what it indicates: it is *relative*, not *absolute* poverty that causes crime. That is, it is the *subjective experience* of poverty that counts and two elements are crucial – the awareness of the fact that you are worse off than others, and the feeling that this is *unjust*. And they add:

> The values of an equal or meritocratic society which capitalism inculcates into people are constantly at loggerheads with the actual material inequalities in the world . . . Crime is endemic to capitalism because it produces both egalitarian ideals and material shortages (ibid, pp. 95–6).

This seems to represent a fusion of anomie and relative deprivation. Is such a view compatible with the postclassical perspective?

In Chapter 5 one of the sources of control that was outlined as part of the postclassical perspective was that of 'belief'; if we believe that the constraints involved in abiding by convention are fair and just we are more likely (though by no means certain) to accept them. This included the requirement that we should feel that the existing social arrangements allow for equal, or justifiably unequal, satisfaction of our needs. A sense of injustice in this respect would leave us feeling freer to indulge our naturally deviant tendencies. This view is entirely compatible with the idea of relative deprivation. The analysis of 'belief' in Chapter 5 concluded that our loss of belief would be contingent on similar conditions to those specified by relative deprivation: knowledge and experience of the fact that we are worse off than others, and the feeling that this is unfair. The postclassical perspective incorporates the idea that the *degree* to which we perceive convention as failing to satisfy our needs will be influenced by the degree to which we perceive that it *does* satisfy the needs of others. This is a necessary condition for us to be able to believe (or not believe) in the justice of convention.

A question that arises is whether inequality is ever likely to be accepted as fair and just by those at the bottom end and, if it is, under what kind of arrangements. This is not, needless to say, a question to which I am likely to give a definitive answer here since it is a question that has engaged social and political philosophers for many centuries, including social contract theorists from the Enlightenment to Rawls (for a useful collection on current debates in the social sciences on 'justice', see Cohen, 1986).

Lea and Young (1984), however, do imply an answer – at least to the first part of the question. Inequality can be made acceptable: 'Exploitative cultures have existed for generations without friction: it is the perception of injustice . . . that counts' (ibid., p. 81). Capitalism, they argue, fails because it *espouses* equality without delivering it. This seems to suggest that it is the strength and consistency of the ideology supporting the inequality that is crucial; if it tells us that the inequality is just, and why it is, we will go along with it. Although they lay great emphasis on the subjective meaning that groups and individuals attach to their experience of inequality, it appears that that subjective meaning can be manipulated by the dominant class.

While allowing that some systems of inequality may be better than others in gaining acceptance, I think the postclassical perspective would present that acceptance as always being somewhat precarious. Our knowledge of the relative degree of conformity under other systems of inequality such as estate and caste systems is inevitably limited and impressionistic. The postclassical perspective would certainly allow that in simple, small-scale societies where the local everyday experience of gross inequality is limited and where the informal sanctions against deviance are powerful, conformity would be likely to be high. Also, the prevalence and effectiveness of the formal enforcement system is a further, independent factor which would lead to considerable variation between different systems. But generally, the postclassical view of human beings as being rationally self-interested would, I think, suggest that they are unlikely to believe in and accept systems of gross, blatant inequality when they are on the receiving end. It may be remembered that one of the difficulties with Beccaria's classical criminology was that he seemed to be unwilling to accept that the logic of his conception of human motivation pointed precisely in this direction: the experience of poverty provided a perfectly 'rational' explanation (in his terms) of the prevalence of property crime among the lower classes. Yet, as we saw, the implications of this were too dangerous for him to feel able to confront.

From the point of view of the postclassical perspective, then, it seems that all grossly unequal societies, where the extent of that inequality is clearly visible to all, are likely to experience difficulties in securing conformity. They are destined either to experience high rates of deviance, or to require the use of a draconian and intrusive enforcement apparatus to gain compliance. The familiar political dilemma posed by these alternatives is a point to which I shall return in the final chapter.

Upper-class Crime

In Chapter 3, when looking at the anti-correctionalist arguments that emerged in the 1960s and 1970s, I dealt briefly with the issue of upper-class or 'white-collar' crime. In that context I was concerned mainly with justifying the correctionalist stance of classical and postclassical criminology. I suggested that the criticism that traditional corrective criminology concentrated on working-class crime at the expense of the more concealed crime of the upper classes amounted to a plea for a massive extension of the correctionalist stance, rather than an argument against it. In the present context, however, this is not sufficient: the acknowledgement of extensive, concealed involvement in crime on the part of the upper classes obviously has serious implications for all criminological theories that explain crime in terms of the experiences and conditions of the lower classes (that is, almost all sociological theories).

It would be useful to review very briefly the claims that have been made with regard to upper-class crime since the resurgence of interest in it in the late 1960s. They amount to an allegation that 'crime' is at least as prevalent among the upper classes but that it tends to take different forms, and that one of the manifestations of the power of this class is that they are able successfully to conceal this prevalence. They are thus guaranteed immunity at all levels: from their actions being *defined* as criminal; from *enforcement* for those actions that are so defined; from the usual adverse social consequences on the rare occasions where criminal conviction does occur.

The first immunity – from definition – is a rather separate argument. The kind of points that have been made here are that the activities of big business in the areas of environmental pollution, excessive profit-making, promotion of harmful products, especially in the Third World, constitute much more serious 'crimes' than those committed by the lower class, and yet are not defined as such (see, for example, Pearce, 1973; Balkan, Berger and Schmidt, 1980). Important as such arguments are, they are cast at the level or moral and political debate about what *ought* to be defined as crime. As such they are rather different from arguments about the prevalence and concealment of actions that *are* defined as crime (though I will be returning later to the importance of this moral and political debate for the postclassical perspective).

The second immunity – from enforcement – has perhaps received the most attention. Particularly singled out have been violations of factory legislation and tax evasion (see Carson, 1970; Leigh, 1980). The studies in these areas have documented the prevalence of such crimes and, more importantly, the way they are concealed by enforcement agencies using informal methods rather than criminal prosecution. It has been pointed out in reply that this does not necessarily indicate that the upper classes are being allowed to get away with their crimes since it could be claimed that the informal procedures that are used are no less effective than prosecution (see Bartrip and Fenn, 1980, on Carson's work; and Leigh himself in Leigh, 1980). However, this does not alter the fact of underrecording and relative injustice when compared with the way lower-class crime is dealt with.

The final immunity is from the usual adverse consequences of criminal conviction, when such conviction does occur. This was well illustrated in one of the seminal cases in the history of 'white-collar crime' in the United States – the so-called 'incredible electrical conspiracy' (violations of the Sherman Act by top executives of the General Electric and Westinghouse companies; see Smith, 1962). Although successfully prosecuted, the offenders received trifling penalties, and managed totally to avoid the stigma of the 'criminal' label with, consequently, no adverse consequences for their subsequent careers. This was a particularly good example of what seems to be a general tendency for the upper classes to be able to present their crimes as if they are merely 'administrative errors' lacking the moral and social qualities of 'real' (working-class) crime (despite much evidence to the contrary).

The weight of the evidence suggests, then, that there is indeed a mass of concealed 'crime' committed by the upper classes which, though different in content, shares all the qualities of lower-class crime. Whether it is on precisely the same scale or not is, of course, impossible to tell. But that does not really alter the challenge it presents to traditional (particularly sociological) theories of crime. How can theories based on the special conditions of lower-class experience explain this category of crime?

The answer is that they cannot. The only way out for them is to provide an entirely separate theory of upper-class crime. Fortunately, this problem does not arise with the postclassical perspective. In fact, it is particularly suited to the explanation of upper-class crime. There is, for example, no problem about motivation: the advantages to be gained from the activities incorporated under the heading of upper-class or white-collar crime are easy to appreciate and, hence, from the assumptions of the postclassical perspective, are already explained. The *extent* of such crime is explained by the nature of the controls. There seems to be no problem here either: the prevalence of such crime that recent research has uncovered is easily explained by the relative weakness of both formal and informal controls. At the formal level, the whole point of much of the research has been to illustrate the relative immunity that the offenders enjoy, as we have seen. At the informal level, the research has shown that such crime does not seem to be accompanied by the same degree of stigma and loss of status among peers as is associated with much conventional crime.

Hagan (1987) has used similar arguments to these to suggest that control theory is particularly suited to the explanation of upper class crime. Using the American 'Watergate' scandal as his example, he concludes:

> The absence of decided public opinion about the seriousness of upperworld deviance, and the weakness of the rules, regulations and checks and balances on the powers and privileges of upperworld citizens, leaves members of the upperworld seductively free to deviate. To ignore this is to ignore a fundamental insight of control theory (ibid., p. 174).

If there is a problem with the way in which both control theory and the postclassical perspective explain upper-class crime it is that, if anything, they appear to explain too much – the 'embarrassment of riches' problem again! As applied here they account for the prevalence, but they do not say anything about the more individual or group characteristics that would explain differences in individual or group participation in such crime (to revert to Hirschi's distinction once again, they explain upper-class *crime* rather than upper-class *criminality*). The reason for this is that there is yet another immunity that the power of such people guarantees – immunity from systematic research. As numerous television and radio enquiry programmes have illustrated, the anonymity and inaccessibility of these figures is legendary. This is likely to remain so. The most that can be said is that the postclassical perspective does seem to make sense of what little we do know.

Finally, there is an important way in which upper-class crime may influence lower-class crime. Matza and others have noted that one of the ways in which offenders justify their offences is by reference to the view that 'everyone is on the fiddle' and mostly getting away with it (see Matza and Sykes's, 1957, 'condemnation of the condemners'). Similarly, in considering the 'belief' source of control earlier, I suggested that in order to believe in and accept the restrictions of convention, we need to feel that others are doing so equally – that we are not being 'mugs'. Lack of this belief enhances the sense of injustice, particularly when the others who are getting away with it are seen as being those who are in power and are the condemners (and prosecutors) of lower-class crime. Ironically, of course, this could be seen as an argument for the *greater* concealment of upper-class crime! Indeed, the argument that it is 'bad for society' for its leaders and top people to be paraded as villains is one that is occasionally heard in certain (usually upper-class) circles.

Race

The assumptions of the postclassical perspective would predict that race would, if anything, be more associated with crime than class is. The well-documented effects of racial discrmination on the objective social and economic position of blacks in Britain and the United States would, alone, lead to the expectation of their having a higher crime rate. Add to this the greater visibility of race and racial discrimination and the sense of exclusion and injustice that it generates and we might expect an even greater lack of commitment to convention among blacks than their objective conditions would predict.

Yet the claim that crime is more prevalent amongst blacks and that it represents a 'problem' requiring attention has been bitterly disputed on the left and in the anti-racist movement. We saw in Chapter 3 how the 'left realist' claim that working-class crime should be treated as a problem by socialists has been heaped with opprobrium by other sections of the left. The same argument in relation to race and crime has been even more ferociously attacked, with the proponents being denounced as racists (see Lea and Young, 1984, the main recipients of such attacks). It is perhaps not difficult to see why this has happened: the argument that black crime is a problem requiring special attention is also the position of the racist far right – although the nature of the problem and its solution are, of course, seen entirely differently.

The arguments against taking black crime seriously are the now familiar ones: that the alleged higher rate is unreal, reflecting selective law enforcement practices by the police and other agents of social control; that anyway, the 'real' crime problem is the concealed crime of the (white) upper classes. On this view, the only 'black crime problem' is that of black people being harassed by racist police (or ignored when they are the victims of white racist attacks).

The counter-arguments are now also familiar. To take the second point first, it has already been repeatedly argued that the undoubted existence of serious, concealed crime among the upper class does not at all constitute an argument for taking *lower*-class crime *less* seriously, especially when it can be shown that lower-class crime consists overwhelmingly of predatory acts against members of its own class. The same point applies equally strongly with reference to race. Despite the undoubted evidence of a growing problem of white racist attacks on blacks in certain parts of this country (and evidence that they are inadequately policed) this does not alter the fact that crime is vastly more *intra*-rather than *inter*-racial (Stevens and Willis, 1979). In other words, black crime *is* a problem, and not because it inconveniences the white upper class (it hardly does at all). It is a problem because it victimises black people.

But is it a 'special' problem? After all, the same prejudice and discrimination that leads to the economic and social disadvantaging of black people might also be expected to lead to their being discriminated against by police, and hence overrepresenting their crime in the official records. This is precisely the argument put forward by the left critics, with numerous incidents of apparently discriminatory actions by police officers to support their claim. However, such incidents do not prove the case that there is *systematic* discrimination sufficient to explain the difference between black and white crime rates. The evidence suggests that police actions are influenced by stereotypes of who they expect to commit crime which are much more varied and general than simply 'black' and 'white', especially in relation to adolescent males (see Roshier and Teff, 1980, Chapter 3). But there are other, more cogent, reasons for being cautious about accepting the 'police bias' argument.

It can equally plausibly be argued that racially prejudiced attitudes and discriminatory actions on the part of the police can lead to *under*representing black crime. The reasoning is as follows: most crime is *intra*-racial; the vast majority of crimes and offenders become known to the police because they are reported to them by victims and witnesses (less than 10 per cent become known through direct police initiatives; see Mawby, 1979). That is, black crime and black criminals become known and recorded mostly through the police taking *black* victims and witnesses seriously. Many police studies have shown that police attitudes to the moral worth of victims and witnesses is an important factor in deciding whether they bother to take action or not (Roshier and Teff, 1980). If they are racially prejudiced, why would they bother to take black victims and witnesses seriously? Some American police studies have suggested that they do not. La Fave (1965) found that the police sometimes took a predominantly 'leave-them-to-it' attitude to high-crime-rate black areas (though they still came out with high rates). As mentioned earlier, much has been recently made of the lack of police action in relation to racially motivated white assaults on blacks (see Lea and Young, 1984); it could well be that, in so far as this is the case, it is part of a more general lack of action on behalf of black victims (*most* of whom are the victims of black offenders). An additional factor, to complicate the picture still further, is that given such attitudes on the part of the police, and the hostility or sense of futility that it can arouse in black victims, the willingness to report crime may be eroded, leading to further *under*recording of (mostly black) crime.

Lea and Young (1984) suggest various other features of crime among black people that do not fit at all well with the view that their higher rate is explained entirely by police prejudice (ibid., pp. 111–12). But what of the data themselves on black and white crime rates? In Britain they do show a considerably higher rate for blacks, though only for those of West Indian rather than Asian origin, and even in their case only in more recent years. Quite apart from the problem of the possible influence of police bias on these figures, there are other difficulties in drawing any direct conclusions from them. For example, it is difficult to work out how much of the difference is due simply to differences in the demographic characteristics of black Britons (age, sex and social class) which are related to crime rates for all races. Exact data on these characteristics are difficult to come by. Nevertheless, those studies that have gone into the data in detail have concluded that the higher black crime rate *cannot* be explained by their different demographic characteristics – that there is an additional 'ethnic factor' (see Rutter and Giller, 1983, pp. 148–55; Stevens and Willis, 1979; and the use of their, and other, data by Lea and Young, 1984).

On the question of the possible effects of police bias, once again the only recourse is to alternative sources of data: self-report and victim studies. The early self-report studies (in the United States) produced an almost exact replication of the findings in relation to social class: the large differences found in the official data were *not* substantiated. There were no significant differences between the self-reported crime rates of blacks and whites. However, later studies cast doubt on these findings. The early studies were based on trivial rather than more serious offences, and the respondents were schoolchildren. As was noted in the previous section on class differences, it is now recognised that such studies as these very much underrepresented serious and habitual offenders. Later, more rigorous, studies *did* confirm the official picture (see Rutter and Giller, 1983).

Victimisation studies in both the United States and Britain (Stevens and Willis, 1979) have usually fairly closely confirmed the officially recorded differences between black and white crime rates. The problem here, however, is that these findings are again open to the possible accusation of bias – that racially prejudiced victims are likely to err, in uncertain circumstances, in favour of perceiving their offenders as being black. However, the weight of evidence overall suggests that this would be extremely unlikely to account for much of the difference and, once again, the tentative conclusions from the surveys of the evidence by Rutter and Giller (1983), Stevens and Willis (1979) and Lea and Young (1984) are that self-report and victim studies support rather than deny the official picture.

It is important to be clear about these conclusions. They are not at all a denial that the criminal justice system may work in a biased and unfavourable manner towards black people. Rather it is saying that such biases work in a complex and contradictory manner as far as the recording of crime rates is concerned, and that they cannot account for the difference between black and white crime rates. As Lea and Young (1984) stress, it is not a matter of a simple either/or choice between 'police bias' and 'real differences'. There is a complex interaction between the two. As they and others (see Roshier and Teff, 1980, Chapter 3) have pointed out, black peoples' perceptions of police discrimination feed their sense of injustice which, in turn, influences their attitudes towards crime and convention as well as their response to the police; these attitudes and responses then naturally influence the reaction of the police towards blacks. The attitudes and behaviour of blacks and police towards each other are thus inextricably tied up with both actual and recorded crime rates.

Although it seems reasonable to conclude that the evidence does support the postclassical expectation of a higher crime rate for blacks, there are some apparent anomalies. The findings do not hold, for example, for Asians; their recorded rates are scarcely any different from those of whites. Nor does the finding hold for *first-generation* West Indian immigrants. Their crime rate has been, if anything, lower than that of the host population. Such anomalies do not necessarily present a problem. As has been pointed out before, the postclassical perspective is not solely dependent on a relationship between social and economic disadvantage in the way that other sociological perspectives have been; other influences may simultaneously be working in the same or contradictory directions.

For example, the difference between Asian and West Indian crime rates is not too difficult to explain. The Asian community incorporates a fairly substantial business and professional class (not very different in proportion to that for whites); combined with the relative cultural separation of the Asian community generally, this provides avenues for conventional need fulfilment that are lacking in the West Indian community. A separate factor, of significance from the point of view of the postclassical perspective, is the difference in the controlling influence of family relationships for the two communities. There is evidence to suggest a substantial degree of homelessness among West Indian origin youths resulting, in part at least, from breakdown in family relationships and children being thrown out by their parents (Pitts, 1986). The effect is to produce a much greater number of youths free from the constraining influence of close family ties than is the case in the Asian community.

The difference between first- and second-generation West Indian crime rates is of particular interest. The high rate only applies to those youths of West Indian origin reared in this country; the original immigrants had a crime rate lower than the host population (see Lambert, 1970). Given the difference in the experience of being reared in the West Indies rather than in Britain, there would be no particular reason to expect that the crime rates of the two generations would be the same. But it does perhaps highlight the significance of racial discrimination in relation to crime. It suggests that it is the direct experience of the injustices, deprivations and exclusions of racial discrimination, rather than simply the fact of being poor and black, that are particularly significant in the failure to commit black youths to convention.

Gender

The analysis so far appears to be in the usual, sexist tradition of criminological work in that it has referred almost exclusively to men's crime. This can be explained by the fact that it has been based on the research undertaken by classical, positivist and interactionist criminologists. They showed little interest in women's crime, and on the few occasions that they did it was usually as an afterthought, based on unexamined assumptions about the differences in women's 'nature' – a good example would be Cohen's (1955) couple of pages on girls' subcultures. However, this explanation is hardly an excuse for perpetuating the bias. In recent times feminist writers have rightly castigated the neglect of women's crime in traditional criminology, and done much to rectify it themselves.

How, then, does the postclassical perspective relate to women's crime? The answer is simple and, I hope, justifies the lack of specific reference to it so far in the development of the perspective. The assumptions about human nature, needs, motivations and sources of control are taken to be as applicable to women as to men. Explanations of differences between men's and women's crime is in terms of the same variables that explain the difference between different men, different classes and different races. And that is *not* in terms of variations in the nature and individual make-up of those individuals and groups, but in terms of the way the sources of control operate in relation to them. As with black peoples' crime, women's crime tends to be associated with the same kinds of variables as white, male crime does. Jensen and Eve (1976, p. 446), for example, looking at female self-reported crime from the point of view of control theory concluded that 'The nature of relationships with other people, institutions and belief systems dwarfs the importance of sex as a variable in the explanation of delinquency .

However, and again the analogy with race and crime is apparent, it is the *differences* in the crime *rates* that presents the challenge to the postclassical perspective. In the case of race, it was the *higher* rate for blacks than for whites that required explanation. In the case of gender, it is the much *lower* rate for women than for men that is the issue. And, again mirroring the argument over race, it is whether this difference can be taken as 'real' that is the starting point.

The gender difference in officially recorded crime rates is of a size and consistency rarely found in criminological research (making its neglect all the more surprising): in both Britain and the United States it has remained for some time at a ratio of about five or six to one (persons found guilty or cautioned). However, just as racism in the administration of criminal justice could be seen to account for the higher rate for blacks, so, too, could sexism be seen to account for the *lower* rate for women. The argument in the latter case has been about 'chivalry' (see Anderson, 1976, for a summary and opposition): that is, that there is a dominant male chivalrous attitude towards women which, in the context of the criminal justice system (mostly administered by males), leads to women being either excluded altogether, or treated leniently when they are prosecuted.

The evidence in favour of chivalry comes, once again, from self-report data (see

Campbell, 1981). They have tended to confirm a significant difference between men's and women's crime, but at a very much reduced level – a ratio of around two to one rather than five or six to one. Again, for the reasons already encountered in relation to class and race, the self-report findings should themselves be viewed with a certain amount of caution. But nevertheless, the comparison certainly suggests a degree of underrecording for women's crime compared with men's, compatible with the chivalry argument. The official data suggests a more lenient attitude to women at subsequent stages of criminal justice processing, too: women are more likely to be cautioned rather than prosecuted, as compared with males, and are less likely to be sent to prison when they are convicted.

Despite the circumstantial support for the chivalry argument, and despite the fact that it is based on the assumption of sexist male attitudes towards women (that they are to be taken less seriously than men), the implication that the criminal justice system is lenient towards women has not always found favour with feminist criminologists. Counter-arguments have often used the dangerous method of generalising from particular instances of undoubtedly sexist decision-making on the part of the magistracy or judiciary. There have also been some notable misinterpretations of the data (see Walker, 1981). One of the most significant of these was by Mawby (1977), who found in his study that a greater proportion of women prisoners were first offenders than was the case with male prisoners. He quite erroneously concluded that this showed that women first offenders are more likely to be sent to prison than are male first offenders (the opposite is in fact the case – see Walker, 1981). Yet this 'finding' has been quoted many times subsequently and appears to have achieved the status of an established fact showing that women are treated more harshly than men.

There is certainly evidence of women being treated particularly harshly by the criminal justice system as *victims* of crime (rape being the obvious example). And in crimes relating to sexual behaviour there is evidence of bias against women. Prostitution, for example, continues to be mostly regarded as a crime on the part of female prostitutes rather than on the part of their male clients, and girls indulging in under-age sex appear to be much more likely to end up in care than are boys doing the same thing (Campbell, 1981). Also, there is evidence to suggest that at least part of the reason for the apparently less harsh treatments meted out to women offenders is that they tend to commit less serious offences (and less serious of their kind), and have fewer previous convictions than male offenders (see Farrington and Morris, 1983). That is, their crimes have more of the characteristics that are associated with lenient treatment generally.

To summarise: the evidence suggests that female crime rates are indeed much lower than male, despite some evidence that the difference may be exaggerated by the effects of more lenient processing by the criminal justice system. If there is more weight to be given to the feminist anti-chivalry arguments than I have allowed, then this would mean that the difference in rates would be greater: it would be closer to the very substantial disparity indicated by the ratio of five or six to one that is found in the official statistics.

So the question that remains to be answered by the postclassical perspective is how this difference can be explained. And a commitment has already been made to an explanation in terms of the same assumptions and variables that the perspective utilises to explain crime generally; there is no question of a reversion to an additional assumption about the 'different nature' of women. The difference between male and female crime rates must reflect the fact that the sources of control operate differently in relation to women, and that such differences in turn reflect their different social position.

Fortunately, the particular features of women's crime seem to lend themselves especially well to explanations in terms of controls. Much of the feminist literature on the social position of women has emphasised the way in which women are much more closely regulated and circumscribed in their opportunities by the variety of informal and formal controls that designate their role. These controls and restrictions could be expected to limit access to and opportunity for criminal activities in much the same way as they limit other activities for women.

For these reasons, control theory has tended to find favour among those criminologists who have addressed themselves to women's crime. Jensen and Eve (1976) have already been mentioned: they found that *combinations* of variables derived from Hirschi's control theory, and other control variables, accounted for much of the difference between male and female delinquency rates. Box (1981), provides evidence to suggest that the three main elements of his version of control theory – social bonding, perception of risk and social/symbolic support – can also account for the difference. He quotes empirical evidence to suggest that girls are more bonded to and controlled by their parents than are boys; that the socialisation pattern and role expectations of girls make them likely to perceive delinquency as less fun and more risky; that female peer-group support is more passive and less supportive of delinquency. Cernkovich and Giordano (1987), in their test of control theory with respect to a wide range of family variables, found that females generally reported much more control than males (females *offenders* rather less so).

Heidensohn (1985), in her comprehensive coverage of the literature on women's crime and the social position of women, also concludes that control theory provides the best account. She illustrates the way in which women are more controlled in the home, at work and in public. In the home they are controlled by the domestic, caring role that is assigned to them (a role that is still to some extent prescribed by gender-differentiated welfare law). At work they are constrained by usually having to sustain the domestic role at the same time as their occupational one. And in public they are subjected to the much more restrictive and passive criteria that define their 'reputation'. Finally, she argues, the male domination of violence (particularly domestic violence) also constitutes an actual or threatened form of control.

The net effect of all of these constraints and controls is to increase the risks of, and decrease the opportunities for, most forms of officially defined crime for women. It is the existence of all these informal, or welfare-law constraints that makes the more overt sanctions of the criminal law *less* necessary to control them, and this is why they appear so much less in the official statistics and in our courts and penal institutions. The gender difference in crime rates fits comfortably with the assumptions and specifications of the postclassical perspective.

Conclusion

The social divisions brought about by age, class, race and gender are important because they influence the relative risks and advantages of crime and conformity for those differentially placed within them. This chapter has suggested that the postclassical perspective can provide an understanding of how these influences work.

Age differences emerged as perhaps the least satisfactorily explained, though not particularly by the postclassical perspective, but by any currently available perspective. Nevertheless, as we saw, a plausible account could be given in postclassical terms, with a suggestion that the explanation is in terms of the differential risks and opportunities associated with different stages in the age-cycle. However, at this stage, it does not seem possible to go much further than that.

Class and race divisions lead to the relative disadvantaging of particular groups in their access to conventional means of satisfying the personal needs that are specified by the postclassical perspective. The emphasis was on *relative* disadvantaging since it is necessary that individuals are *aware* of their disadvantaging (through direct experience of their position relative to the position of others). This introduced the significance of 'belief' as a source of control since it is also the perception of their relative disadvantaging as being *unjust* that is crucial in reducing individuals' commitment to convention. It was suggested that the postclassical perspective implied that all forms of gross and apparent inequality would be likely to lead to problems in gaining the compliance of those at the bottom of the heap.

The gender division raised different issues, though the explanation of the particular features of women's crime was again in terms of the relative risks and advantages specified by the postclassical perspective. The lower rate of recorded crime for women was explained by a different kind of disadvantaging: the higher risks that are involved in non-conformity as a result of the more restricted and controlled position of women.

The family and community factors dealt with in Chapter 6 – the formation of affectional ties, the social definition of 'ability' and its consequences, the influences of school, peers and neighbourhood – are clearly related to and influenced by these social divisions, but they are not simply reducible to them; within each class, race or gender these family and community factors still differentiate between individuals in terms of their involvement in crime. This point was incorporated into the reformulation of anomie theory, enabling it to encompass any kind of barrier – not just class – that may restrict access to conventional forms of need satisfaction.

8 Contexts of Control, III: The Criminal Justice System and Crime-Prevention Policy

Classical criminologists saw the success of crime control as being almost exclusively a function of the efficiency of the criminal justice system. As was noted earlier, this was a curiously narrow view, even in terms of their own perspective. Their conception of human beings as naturally deviant, rationally weighing up the pros and cons of crime as against conformity, clearly suggests a much wider set of influences on our decisions than simply our perceptions of the criminal justice system. To rectify that omission, I have so far been exclusively concerned with these other influences. It now remains to consider the part played by the criminal justice system in the postclassical perspective.

The sources of control and the underlying needs they relate to, which have formed the basis of the postclassical version of crime control, are recognised by most penal systems. That is, most penal punishments consist of the denial, or threat of denial, of our basic requirements for status, autonomy, security, money, reputation and self-esteem. In that sense, they fit well with the postclassical perspective; they acknowledge its assumptions. But despite that, and in gross contradiction to the original classical view, all the evidence suggests that criminal justice systems play a minor role in controlling crime. The enormous differences in crime rates between different societies, or between different periods of time in the same societies, do not relate at all well to differences in the nature and content of criminal justice systems. Nor have any changes that have been made to penal methods, with a view to reducing crime, ever been clearly established as having achieved that end. Few contemporary criminologists would now deny that the major determinants of crime rates lie outside of the realm of penal policy, in the wider social, political and economic context.

This seems a rather dismissive starting point. However, it is not to suggest that the criminal justice system plays no part at all (or that we can do without it!). Rather, it is to suggest that the tendency to view the 'crime problem' as a 'penal' problem is very much mistaken, and that experience shows that we should never usually expect to be able to achieve more than fairly limited effects on the extent of crime through penal policy. More importantly, given this humility with respect to crime control, it allows that other expectations of the criminal justice system may be given correspondingly more importance – such as, for example, that it be fair and humane.

In the previous chapters, especially Chapter 3, issues relating to penal and crime-prevention policy have arisen at several points, and a series of loose ends have been left untied. These need now to be sorted out if a coherent postclassical perspective is to be developed. Broadly, they come under two headings: problems of 'correction'; and problems of 'justice'. On the first, some considerable time was spent in Chapter 3 justifying the 'correctionalist' stance against the various attacks that had been made against it. But the evidence on the effectiveness of the classical version of correction – deterrence – was left unexamined. Also, it was promised that something would be done about the contradiction between the (classical) deterrent claim for the criminal justice system and the 'labelling' theory of the interactionists. Under the second heading, the fundamental incompatibility between 'correction' and 'justice' as penal aims will be considered. Finally, some conclusions will be drawn for a postclassical penal policy.

Correction

Before considering what kind of correctionalist aims are appropriate for the criminal justice system under the postclassical perspective it is necessary to consider whether we can expect it to be correctionalist at all. Interactionists and labelling theorists claimed that, if anything, it can only make things worse. Lemert's (1967) distinction between primary and secondary deviation (see Chapter 3) suggested that the main effect of formal processing is to produce isolation from convention, an alteration in self-conception and subsequently *more* deviation than would otherwise have been the case. It was pointed out in the earlier discussion that it is difficult to take this argument seriously if it is claiming that such consequences are *inevitable* (for example, it is actually the case that the majority of people officially 'labelled' for the first time are never labelled again). But there is plenty of evidence to suggest that it does sometimes have this effect. The problem with interactionism and labelling theory is that they did not tell us under what circumstances we might and might not expect it.

The postclassical perspective may be able to help here. Its assumptions would suggest that we might expect two diametrically opposed sets of consequences resulting from the operations of the criminal justice system. On the one hand, it would predict that fear of the available sanctions (or of their repetition once experienced) would commit people to conformity. That is, it can warn us, or remind us, of what we have to lose. On the other hand, the stigmatising effects of being officially labelled can also have the effect of closing off access to legitimate opportunities; they can also lead to the acquisition of deviant associates supportive of deviation. In other words, the effects of official processing can also be to create a situation (and draw your attention to that situation) where you do *not* have much to lose through deviation.

The problem with the criminal justice system is precisely the fact, mentioned earlier, that it plays on the basic needs and requirements that constitute the 'sources of control' under the postclassical perspective. It works by threatening those needs. Consequently, when its sanctions are actually enforced, it can damage our conventional sources of need fulfilment (for example by severing our affectional ties, damaging our conventional reputation, reducing our wealth). In this respect, it is rather like deterrence theories in other realms (for example, the nuclear deterrent), in that it relies on the effectiveness of the *threat*; the *actualisation* of the threat tends to destroy the whole objective of the deterrent exercise (though, of course, this is much more extreme in the case of the nuclear deterrent!). In the case of the penal deterrent, it is more to the point to draw attention to the simultaneous, contradictory forces at work. However, to anticipate something that will be discussed later, the argument here suggests that it is likely to be the perceived strength of the threat, rather than its actualisation, that will be the most effective in controlling crime.

Given these contradictory forces at work in the operation of the criminal justice system, how are they likely to resolve themselves in individual instances? The postclassical perspective suggests an answer in terms of the prior level of commitment to convention that characterises different individuals when they experience penal sanctions. The experience can have entirely different meanings for different individuals when this is taken into account.

The postclassical view is that everyone is capable of criminal acts. Consequently, perhaps the majority of criminal acts (particularly first offences) are committed by people who in most respects are still committed to convention. That is, they are occasional, situational offences, not committed by individuals with any deep-seated problems of satisfying their needs via conventional avenues. The stake in conformity of these, the majority of offenders, is such that the experience of the penal sanction confronts them with what they stand to lose; this is more than sufficient to counteract any 'closing-off' effects that the stigma of the sanction may involve (usually fairly minimal for most first offences). The net effect is most likely to be a push towards conformity.

For those whose commitments to convention are already low (for reasons related to the other, non-penal variables dealt with in the preceding chapters) the experience of the criminal sanction may have a quite different impact. For them, convention already appears to offer little. The addition of the stigmatising consequences of the sanction, even when fairly limited, may simply make convention appear to offer still less. As they progress up the penal tariff via subsequent convictions this effect becomes more and more marked, as witnessed by the universally found penological fact that the more previous convictions offenders have, the more likely they are to commit further offences, regardless of what kind of punishment is meted out to them.

If this analysis has some force, then the contradictory factors at work in the penal process are likely to resolve themselves in varied, complex ways in individual cases. However, this conclusion does not rule out the possibility of the criminal justice system having a *generally* deterrent effect for most people. And this, of course, is one of the premises on which it operates and which was taken for granted by the original classical criminologists. Bearing in mind the scepticism that we encountered in Chapter 3 about the general effectiveness of *rehabilitation* as a penal aim, what is the evidence in relation to deterrence?

In the early 1970s, and partly as a result of a resurgence of interest in classical, 'rational choice' models of human action, there was an increased output of research on deterrence (Zimring and Hawkins, 1973; Andenaes, 1974; Gibbs, 1975). Some of this came from more politically conservative quarters and challenged what had been a kind of liberal-academic consensus denying the 'special' effectiveness of overtly deterrent sentences. Even capital punishment found new favour (see Ehrlich, 1975, though he in turn 'has been the subject of telling criticism', as Walker, 1985, p. 95, put it). Needless to say, these arguments have generated some complex definitional and methodological problems and not much consensus. However, it is permissible to suggest a few tentative conclusions.

First, most would agree with the general point that the existence of some kind of threat of some kind of punishment from some kind of criminal justice system does deter crime. The often-quoted example of the period when there was no police force in action in Nazi-occupied Denmark (Andenaes, 1974) suggests that the disappearance of the threat of penal sanctions is accompanied by very considerable increases in crime (though not, apparently, for all categories – at least in the short run). As Walker (1985, p. 94) points out, over-enthusiastic opponents of deterrence have tended to misrepresent the issue in such pronouncements as 'capital punishment does not act as a deterrent'. The most that can actually be concluded from the evidence is that capital punishment is no *more* deterrent than its alternatives (which are themselves usually fairly draconian), certainly not that it does not act as a deterrent at all.

Second, the evidence on whether variations in the *severity* of deterrent punishments influence crime rates is much more equivocal. As Walker (1985, p. 99) points out, the evidence is often 'anecdotal and weak'. Even those analysts who have concluded that there is, or may be, some relationship (Walker, 1985; Rutter and Giller, 1983) have done so with many qualifications and limitations. One of the limitations is that in practice sentencers are usually unwilling to apply what they regard as disproportionately severe sentences. This means that comparisons are only possible across a fairly narrow range of alternatives (in terms of severity) for particular offences. We do not know, for example, whether on-the-spot floggings for parking offences would be particularly effective – hopefully because we would never want to! But it may well be that because, for moral and humane reasons, the range of choice in the severity of sentences is always limited, the possibilities for altering crime rates by this method are always likely to be equally limited.

Finally, the findings relating to the effects of increasing both the objective likelihood, and the subjective perception of the likelihood, of being apprehended have been much more promising than the findings relating to increasing the severity of punishments. Indeed, it was noted in Chapter 3 (in the discussion of control theory) that the upsurge of interest in the classical perspective that took place in the 1970s seems to have resolved itself almost entirely into a 'situational' or 'rational-choice' model, that is, a concern with controlling crime through decreasing the opportunities (by crime-prevention policy to encourage such things as the better protection of property), and through increasing the risk of detection (through more efficient policing and encouraging public self-surveillance by, for example, environmental design). The strength of these arguments lies in the fact that they have been based on reasonably well-documented evidence of modestly beneficial results, and that their programmes are limited and practicable.

However, relatively harmless as such approaches appear to be, they are not ideologically uncontentious. Some observers have seen the concern with better policing, protection and surveillance as part of a wider spreading of the state's 'net' (net analogies seem to be popular – see Cohen, 1985, the most eloquent proponent). This view, however, does not seem to be entirely fair. In practice, the imposition of more external surveillance, intervention and control is an expensive and inefficient method of gaining compliance. It was noted in the discussion of race and crime in the previous chapter that the police are almost entirely dependent on the vigilance and co-operation of the community they are policing to report incidents and supply them with the necessary information they need to apprehend offenders. For this purely practical reason efficient crime control is difficult to impose by external forces on an unwilling populace. As Wilson (1975) and others (see particularly Nieburg, 1974) have been quick to point out, the community itself constitutes the 'front line' of the deterrent. It is not just the efficiency and ubiquity of the police that reduces impunity, it is more importantly the knowledge and expectation that they will be summoned by victims, witnesses and passers-by.

However, this does not entirely dispel the 'Big Brother' imagery invoked by Cohen. Community 'self-policing' could be seen simply as another manifestation of it. Commenting on the low rate of crime in Japan, Whymant (1975, p. 12) put it down at least partly to the 'very special relationship between police and community, a relationship nursed with tenderness by the police', but adds that 'the price of freedom from crime is eternal vigilance that sometimes borders on prying that people in Britain might well resent. Here it is acceptable: the concept of privacy does not exist, and the Japanese have no word for it.'

I argued in Chapter 4 (and Matthews and Young, 1986, have made the same point) that the sole concentration on risk and opportunity factors, though certainly realistic in practical terms, has drastically narrowed the context of intellectual debate in relation to crime. I have further argued that it also constitutes an unwarranted restriction of the classical perspective (which the postclassical perspective is an attempt to rectify). However, it cannot be denied that it is still undoubtedly in keeping with that perspective, and must be considered a valuable part of it. It is also perhaps worth adding that it has also provided a service in diverting the concern with deterrence away from the traditional preoccupation with harsh punishment.

Justice

The greatest problem with correction as a penal aim, whether in its deterrent or rehabilitative form, is that it is incompatible with another requirement that most people consider to be equally important: justice. In this context justice implies two interrelated ideas: equality (equally culpable offenders should be punished equally) and proportionality (the severity of the punishment should be proportional to the wickedness of the offence). Efficient deterrence or rehabilitation do not necessarily require either and, as we have already seen, this has led them both into deep trouble. In Chapter 3 we saw how the overriding of these principles gave rise to an academic revolt against rehabilitation. And in Chapter 1 we saw that, although Beccaria accepted the principle of proportionality (on deterrent rather than justice grounds), his attempt to eliminate questions of individual culpability proved unacceptable in practice and gave rise to the neoclassical compromise.

Where does the postclassical perspective stand on this issue? Its classical origins and commitment to crime control appear to push it into unavoidable conflict with the principles of justice. There does not seem to be any room for principles which so obviously relate to irrational internal feelings (always open to being unflatteringly construed as those of 'vengeance').

Yet it is not as simple as that. Even in the original classical position there is a rather ambiguous view of our rationality. The social contract portrays us as both self-seeking and yet able to appreciate the mutual (and hence ultimately individual) advantages of restraint. In the postclassical perspective it has already been emphasised, when considering economic advantage and disadvantage, that our feelings about the justice of the restraints involved in adhering to convention are vital in influencing the extent of our compliance. The same will surely apply to our feelings about the operations of the criminal justice system; whether or not we see it as just is hence an important *practical* consideration.

As long as people hold each other to be responsible for their actions (and there is little sign of them not doing so, despite the long opposition from positivists), and as long as penal systems punish people (and there is no sign of that changing either, despite the attempt by some rehabilitationists to call punishment something else) then *it is likely that people will demand proportionality between punishments and offences*. Without proportionality criminal justice systems will not be perceived as just. And if there is no sense of justice then deterrence, rehabilitation or any other corrective penal aim will be undermined. Beccaria, it may be remembered, avoided the difficult practical issue that this raises by accepting the necessity for proportionality, but on the wholly unwarranted grounds that it would guarantee the most effective *deterrence*. He was right to assume that it was necessary in order to be effective, but wrong in assuming that this was for deterrent reasons.

However, despite this claim of practical effectiveness, proportionality involves primarily *moral* considerations: issues of the 'harmfulness' of acts and the 'culpability' of offenders. This underlines an important point about the postclassical perspective that differentiates it from both positivism and its classical predecessor: the acknowledgement that crime is a *moral*, and not a purely *technical*, issue. As was made clear in Chapter 4, crimes are *not* acts that can be defined in terms of their objective harmfulness. Rather, they involve inter-subjective assessments of goodness and badness. It is for this reason that the issue of crime cannot avoid moral debates about which acts are bad, how bad some are compared with others and how culpable people are who commit them. Crime is ultimately a moral and political issue, not a scientific and technical one.

Justice is not only a question of proportionality. It is also an issue of equality, in the sense that it requires that equally culpable offenders should be punished equally. This reintroduces several arguments that we have already encountered. It requires, for example, that class, race and gender differences should not influence either the definition or enforcement of legal rules, since they are not 'relevant' differences in terms of culpability. The question of upper-class crime discussed in Chapter 7 (that is, that equally 'bad' acts committed by the powerful are either not defined or not treated as crimes) is therefore an issue that must be confronted in considering the likely corrective effectiveness of criminal justice systems.

Justice interconnects with efficiency. Inefficiency in criminal justice systems creates its own sense of injustice. For example, I may feel that it is reasonable to be expected to pay my television licence and that those who are apprehended for not doing so are treated impartially. If, however, most people are getting away with not paying it, I will feel a sense of unfairness in doing so myself. High levels of impunity are thus important not just because they reduce the sense of risk, but also because they create a sense of unjust personal sacrifice in those who wish to comply. Feeling a mug is one important aspect of the sense of injustice.

For all these reasons, and despite the apparent inconsistency for a classically based, avowedly correctionalist criminology, there is a strong argument for justice as the focal concern of a postclassical criminal justice system. I have been able to claim *practical* grounds for this conclusion because there are no demonstrably successful corrective programmes based on the alternative principles of individualised treatment (whether deterrent or rehabilitative). Consequently, it is reasonable to assume that the losses in commitment that would be generated through the inherent injustice involved in following these alternative principles would always outweigh any practical benefits.

Conclusion: Postclassical Criminal Justice

Bearing in mind the general points covered so far in the discussion of correction and justice, it remains to summarise the basic principles of a criminal justice system compatible with the postclassical perspective.

First, as the previous section has made clear, the fundamental consideration must be justice. To be just, the criminal justice system must be impartial in its definition and enforcement of legal rules (which means it must also be reasonably efficient), and it must equate the severity of its punishments with the evil of the offence and the culpability of the offender (based on some kind of notional tariff). These requirements can only be satisfied through a process of moral debate. And since, to be effective, they must satisfy public feeling on these matters, the moral debate must ultimately be a public, democratic one. Questions of what should be defined as crimes, and their relative seriousness, must be open to public access and review via the political process. Above all, the moral and political nature of the debate means that the main contours of the criminal justice system *cannot* be established by 'technical experts', simply because the issues are not, fundamentally, technical ones.

It has been acknowledged that this seems to be a strangely irrational starting point for a perspective rooted in the classical tradition of Beccaria. But I have argued that it is in fact in keeping with the traditional concern with efficient crime control since correctionalist programmes will always be self-defeating unless they are seen to be just by those they deal with. But it also appears to be out of keeping with the classical tradition for other reasons. For example, retributive justice (which this is) is associated with harshness and cruelty rather than the humanity of Beccaria (though see Chapter 1 on this point). Also, whatever sense of justice the retributive tariff may impart, the punishments themselves seem peculiarly pointless and irrational – not apparently concerned with any benefits for offenders, victims or society.

The accusation of harshness and cruelty is not really fair to retributive justice. In fact, the retributive principle of proportionality says nothing about the *general level* of punishment. It is as well satisfied by a tariff of graduated fines as it is by one of physical punishments or terms of imprisonment. The argument that punishments are unfairly severe is just as retributive in nature as the argument that they are not punitive enough. However, the requirement that public moral attitudes need to be reflected if the system is to be perceived as just does not augur well for mild punishments, given the high degree of public support for corporal and capital punishment that still seems to persist. But that problem applies equally to other penal aims – there is equally widespread belief in the *deterrent* effect of harsh punishment, for example. Retributive justice does not automatically require a higher level of severity than any other penal aim.

Beccaria (despite my reservations about the ultimate humanity of his programme), in his section on 'Mildness of Punishments' still provides the most eloquent arguments against severity and cruelty – much of it as applicable here as to his own version of criminal justice. For example:

In proportion as torments become more cruel, the spirits of men, which are like fluids that always rise to the level of surrounding objects, become callous, and the ever lively force of the passions brings it to pass that after a hundred years of cruel torments the wheel inspires no greater fear than imprisonment once did . . . The countries and times most notorious for severity of penalties have always been those in which the bloodiest and most inhumane of deeds were committed, for the same spirit of ferocity that guided the hand of the legislators also ruled that of the parricide and assassin (Beccaria, 1963, pp. 43–4)

In addition to harshness and cruelty, the other criticism of retributive justice mentioned above was that it seems to involve irrational, pointless punishment, without any socially useful purpose (since even though I have argued that it provides as good a basis as any for crime control, that is not its essential purpose). The main aim of retributive justice is to equate suffering with culpability. Worse, the guiding sentiment of this exercise appears to be reducible to something particularly irrational and pointless – vengeance.

Philosophers have long been concerned with producing a rather more acceptable justification for retributive justice than vengeance (see Ten, 1987, Chapter 3, for a useful analysis). A notable, recent example is that of Nozick (1981). Nozick proposes five crucial differences: revenge may be exacted for any kind of injury, harm or slight, retribution only for a moral wrong; retribution is limited (by proportionality), revenge is unlimited (except by the satisfaction of the avenger); revenge is personal, while retribution may be administered impersonally; revenge involves the derivation of pleasure from the inflicted suffering, retribution does not; revenge is not principled like retribution, as it does not involve the avenger acting similarly in similar circumstances.

If we accept Nozick's distinctions and absolve retribution from being guilty of revenge, the question arises why it *does* involve punishment, and why *proportional* punishment. These questions still need to be answered if it is to avoid the charge of pointlessness and irrationality. Fortunately, once again this is a question that has received considerable philosophical attention. Much the best justification, it seems to me (and see Finnis, 1968; Morris, 1973; Ten, 1987), is that punishment is for the purpose of *rectifying unfairness to law-abiding citizens.*

Under this heading punishment is justified on the grounds that the offender has taken an unfair advantage over law-abiding citizens (to be unfair, it must be the case that it was undertaken *voluntarily*). This is because to be law-abiding is to exercise self-restraint (as is recognised in both the classical and postclassical perspectives). The aim of punishment is thus to restore the balance of benefits and obligations that the offender's act upset. The unfair advantage gained by the offender does not consist of the material benefits gained through the act. Rather, the advantage consists of the *voluntary renunciation of the burden of restraining oneself.* The offender's benefit is the degree of unfair advantage taken, and this is proportional to the contribution that the particular violated law makes to the well-being of everyone. More grave offences make a greater contribution than less grave ones (that is what 'grave' is taken to mean) – hence the punishment must be proportional to the gravity of the offence.

This seems to provide a rather healthier-looking and rational basis for retribution (and without slipping into some disguised claim for its special effectiveness in crime control; the justification is still in terms of justice). But there is still a problem: as a justification it takes no account of the practical, socio-economic circumstances in which crime takes place. As Ten points out (though he still favours this particular justification) it is based on the assumption that a (our) system of law, if complied with, *benefits every one equally*; it ignores socio-economic disadvantages. Thus, it is argued, even if our legal rules were genuinely impartial, in a formal sense, in their definition and enforcement (as specified in the previous section) in an unequal society they would still be unjust *in their consequences*. As leftist critics reasonably ask of justice models, how is it *possible* to be just in an unjust society (such as our own)?

Fortunately, it seems to me, the answer to this question is fairly straightforward; it cannot be, and it is absurd to expect that the criminal justice system should be. This is because (and this is one of the fundamental premises of the postclassical perspective) the causes and correction of crime are largely beyond the scope of criminal justice systems; they are primarily influenced by fundamental social and economic processes. It is only states, through the social and economic policies they promote, that can achieve these ends. If states pursue criminogenic policies, there is nothing much that criminal justice systems can do about it; if states pursue unjust policies, there is nothing much they can do about that either. The reasons, in the latter case, are rather different; criminal justice systems are set up by and financed by states. It is consequently logically absurd to expect, in any society, that they would be able systematically and effectively to undermine and ameliorate the injustices promoted by the state. I say 'systematically and effectively' since there are, of course, numerous heroic examples of attempts and achievements falling short of those criteria.

In unjust societies, then, criminal justice systems pursuing justice in terms of the criteria outlined above will also be unjust. I have, however, overstated the case in saying *nothing* can be expected to be done about this. There is *some* room for manoeuvre. For example, proportionality, requiring the balancing of culpability with punishment, allows socio-economic factors to be introduced as factors influencing the 'received' severity of punishment (a good example would be the argument that fines should be means-tested, as in Sweden). Nevertheless, I would still maintain that criminal justice systems should work on the assumption that laws benefit, and apply to, everyone equally, and that arguments about whether they do or not, and what should be done about it, should be aimed at those who define the legal rules and the social and economic context in which they operate, that is, the state and its agencies and the political processes that bring them about.

This stance would, admittedly, be much more embarrassing to sustain if crime in our society consisted mainly of a heroic struggle on the part of the disadvantaged to right wrongs and bring about justice. It has been strongly argued throughout that this is in fact rarely the case. Despite the fact that crime can often be seen to be rooted in disadvantage and injustice, it tends to take a form that is as inappropriate and unacceptable to social reformers as it is to conservatives. But even if crime *was* predominantly of the heroic struggle variety it would still, for the reasons outlined above, be totally unrealistic to imagine that this could be recognised, or promoted by criminal justice systems.

A further problem remains. So far the concern has been to rescue retributive justice from accusations of harshness, cruelty and irrationality. Even if this could be considered successful, it still remains the case that the sole concern with justice leaves no room for any practical, socially useful objectives in relation to crime.

For this reason, perhaps, the academic revolt against rehabilitation has been accompanied by interest in objectives other than simply a 'return to justice' – for example, compensation and restitution (see Chapter 3). These aims can be easily incorporated into the framework of the retributive tariff: the principles of proportionality and culpability can be used to determine the amount of compensation or restitution to be paid or earned by offenders. This would enable socially useful objectives to accompany the sense of justice. There is also evidence to suggest that this approach has considerable popular support (see Hough and Moxon, 1985). However, useful as these additions are, they are unlikely ever to be universally applicable. Many offences and offenders do not lend themselves easily to the principles of compensation and restitution. Even fines, which could be construed as a very general and indirect form of compensation payment (to the state), are limited in their applicability by the ability of offenders to pay (as witnessed by the number of fine defaulters in our prisons). Making people work to earn their compensation or restitution payments involves a relatively high degree of intervention in their lives, often not warranted on retributive grounds, and raises many other difficulties during periods of high unemployment.

Nevertheless, within the justice framework, which sets the degree of punishment (or rather, in the case of the vast bulk of trivial offences, the degree of inconvenience) according to the gravity of the offence, there is plenty of room to pursue these more constructive objectives in the actual *content* of the punishments or inconveniences that are utilised. Indeed, a shift of attention to the practical needs of victims of offences (in the form of compensation and restitution schemes) has been, and continues to be, a significant trend in recent criminal justice developments in this country (see Bottoms, 1983).

Given this fundamental commitment of the postclassical perspective to justice incorporating, where practicable, restitution and compensation, what of the traditional, directly correctionalist aims of deterrence and rehabilitation – are they to be ignored altogether?

As far as deterrence is concerned, we can return to Beccaria and accept that proportionality will guarantee adequate deterrence. It has been acknowledged that the existence of the criminal justice system has *some* deterrent effect and, since we do not know what is specially deterrent, a system based on proportionality is likely to be as effective in this respect as anything else would be. Unlike Beccaria, of course, the postclassical position justifies proportionality in terms of the practical consequences of the sense of justice it generates, not by claiming special deterrent effects. Deterrence, it was concluded, depends much more on people's perceptions of their probability of being apprehended than on the specific nature of the punishments involved.

It was pointed out in chapter 1 that despite Beccaria's concentration on deterrence, the classical commitment to correction was also compatible with rehabilitation. Indeed, both Beccaria and Bentham saw insight and rationality acquired through education as a means of controlling crime, and this has much in common with the individual and group therapy and educational programmes that have been advocated and used by rehabilitationists. The great weakness in the argument, however, is the assumption that insight and rationality would guarantee conformity. Given the classical assumptions about the nature of human beings, the objective position of deprivation that people find themselves in plus the often low probability of apprehension would suggest precisely the opposite: crime would be an extremely rational choice. As we have seen before, the logic of this argument was evaded by Beccaria, probably because of its dangerous political implications.

Rehabilitation, however, has other serious problems and we saw in Chapter 3 how these have led to its widespread rejection in academic circles. In summary, the opposition is based on the argument that it has licensed greater intervention in offenders' lives than would be warranted on 'justice' grounds, and without any evidence to support its rehabilitative claims. For these reasons it is also unacceptable to postclassical criminology. This would not, of course, rule out rehabilitative programmes being offered, on a genuinely voluntary basis, to offenders. But they would have to be within the confines of sentences based on justice criteria; they would never be allowed to determine the nature of sentences. This would naturally mean the abolition of all indeterminate elements in sentencing, including parole. Quite apart from being based on spurious rehabilitative claims, they have been the cause of a widespread sense of injustice within the criminal justice system.

Finally, in view of the limited success that can be expected from trying to control crime through changes in the criminal justice system, it is perhaps not surprising that the focus of those criminologists concerned with practical crime control has become narrower and narrower. As we have seen, it first led them to reject almost all previous sociological and psychological theories about the causes of crime since they dealt with individual, social or economic factors that were beyond the reach of crime-control strategists. Next, the criminal justice system appears not to be amenable to demonstrably successful grand strategies. All that seems to be left are the neighbourhood crime-prevention and surveillance strategies that have become the main interest of 'situational' or 'rational-choice' criminologists. This is not to belittle these developments. As I have acknowledged, they are a logical development of classical principles. Nor can their logic be faulted in terms of what is realistically achievable for those genuinely concerned with promoting practical crime-control strategies. But the main argument of this book has been that, despite the fact that Beccaria himself was partly responsible for setting a narrow focus for the classical perspective, it would be a pity, and intellectually unsatisfactory, to leave that perspective undeveloped and unexamined by restricting it to immediately practicable objectives.

9 Conclusions: The Politics of Crime Control

At the most general level, thinking about crime and its control over the past two hundred years has fallen into two broad frameworks: the socio-cultural and the individual. In the first, the nature and extent of crime is seen as being primarily a function of social, economic and political arrangements. Although the formal procedures for processing, punishing or treating individual offenders (the criminal justice system) form part of these arrangements, they tend not to be the main concern within this framework. Instead, the debate about controlling crime overlaps with the wider ideological debate about the 'good' society (in fact, there is sometimes a danger of its being 'lost', as a specific concern, within that debate – as we saw in the discussion of Marxist criminology).

In the second (the 'individual') framework, crime is seen primarily as an expression of individual characteristics. It results either from special wickedness (to be controlled by effective punishment) or from individual pathology (to be controlled by effective diagnosis and individualised treatment). Either way, the focus tends to be on the nature and operation of the criminal justice system as a means of controlling crime; the wider socio-cultural context tends to be ignored.

Needless to say, as in the case of all dichotomies, particular instances recalcitrantly refuse to fit into their proper places. One of the oddities noted in Chapter 2 was that sociological theorists, who saw crime as a rational response to the thwarting of conventional ambitions by social and economic inequalities, nevertheless tended to see its *control* in terms of individual rehabilitation! However, rather than denying the usefulness of the dichotomy, I would suggest (and the point will be developed below) that this example rather indicates the powerful political pressures pushing towards the 'individual' framework, even where it defies the logic of the explanatory theory.

Despite the scepticism expressed in Chapter 3 about over-enthusiastic 'politicising' of crime, the postclassical perspective offered in this book is very much in the socio-cultural framework. It starts from the assumption (see Jencks, 1987) that differences between societies, in terms of their internal social and economic arrangements, have far more effect on crime rates than do differences between individuals. While this does not eliminate the possible significance of individual differences, it does suggest that the socio-cultural framework is likely to be a much more fruitful one for understanding the prevalence and control of crime. However, as the previous chapters have suggested, the evidence does not lend much support to the belief that this understanding is likely to be in terms of grand-scale ideological blueprints. Crime does not, for example, appear to be simply a function of the mode of production: societies with the same (capitalist) mode of production have dramatically different crime rates (Clinard, 1978) and there are no examples of alternative modes having transformed them.

Like its classical ancestor, the postclassical perspective sees the problem of crime as a problem of conformity. It asks what it is that influences us to comply with rules which (however they are defined) are incompatible with the direct pursuit of our personal interests. At the most general level, the answer has been that it depends on the extent to which we see conformity as allowing the satisfaction of our basic needs, and deviation leading to their denial. The more detailed analysis has been concerned with the way in which our expectations in these respects are influenced by family, school, peer and neighbourhood factors, and by the social consequences of our class, race, gender and age-group membership.

If it were possible to generalise the conclusions of this analysis, it would involve the use of a familiar distinction in sociology: that between 'insiders' and 'outsiders'. The privileges and rewards of being an insider in any group or setting (whether family, peer-group, neighbourhood or society) provide perhaps the greatest incentive to conform to its strictures. Being an outsider does not motivate us to deviate; it simply releases us from any sense of obligation to conform.

The privileges and rewards of being an insider consist of the sense that our basic needs are being satisfied. Or rather, it is the sense that they are being *relatively well* satisfied. An important proviso throughout has been that our sense of satisfaction is always dependent, to some extent at least, on what we perceive as *possible* in terms of visible alternatives. Of particular importance, it seems, is the extent to which our primary associations in the family, school, peer group and neighbourhood provide us with affection and status (as defined in Chapter 4) and the extent to which they are manipulated for the purposes of gaining compliance with what is defined as conformity. However, 'higher-level' factors (such as class, race and gender) have also been seen to play a part, both in terms of their direct social consequences in relation to need satisfaction, and through their influence on the nature and quality of the satisfactions possible at the family and community level.

Being an insider, however, is not all 'good'. It may also involve what some would regard as oppression and isolation from desirable alternatives. For example, the low rate of crime for women, it was argued, stems at least partly from the especially restrictive control of women that feminists are fighting against. But this simply illustrates a much wider issue which, again, has been fundamental to the postclassical perspective: the rules that define conformity are relative, not absolute and therefore conformity is only 'good' to the extent that we regard the rules as 'good'. That is, crime and conformity are ultimately moral and not technical issues.

Outsiders may consist of individuals within lower-level settings such as the family, and of whole groups in relation to the society generally. Outsider groups still, of course, face the problem of *internal* compliance. But the problem is the same; it is a matter of how far individual needs are satisfied within the group, and of the risks contingent on deviation. The level of compliance of outsider groups in relation to the societies in which they are outsiders is much more of a problem. The absence of incentives in terms of need satisfaction means that the overall level of compliance will be a function of two factors. The first is the effectiveness (mostly in terms of perceived certainty) of the punishment system. The more *effectively* totalitarian the regime, the greater this is likely to be. The second is the extent to which the group is isolated from direct experience of its relative disadvantage in relation to the host culture (that is, the extent of the routine experience and hence awareness of the outsider status). Belief, as one of the sources of control discussed in Chapter 4, plays an important part here. The degree of isolation from alternative belief systems to the self-justificatory one of the dominant culture, also plays a part. I have argued, however, that both of these forms of control are relatively insecure and unstable compared with *insider* status.

When deviation takes a group form, there is a tendency for a confusion to arise as to the boundary between *criminal* and *political* activity. The next, and final, section will return to this issue in the context of a more general discussion of the politics of crime control.

The Politics of Crime Control

Given the apparent empirical support for the socio-cultural framework for understanding crime and its control, and given the relatively limited role that seems to be applicable to the criminal justice system, it must be acknowledged that the former has been singularly unsuccessful both historically and currently in gaining recognition from either the public or politicians. Crime and its control almost always has been, and continues to be, regarded as a problem of individuals going wrong and requiring punishment or treatment from the criminal justice system. If there is a 'crime problem', then it is invariably seen as a problem for that system. This has not been helped by the fact that criminological theorists have tended to go along with this, sometimes even when, as noted above in the case of sociological positivists, their theories pointed in the opposite direction.

One fairly straightforward reason for this state of affairs is that it is the criminal justice system that defines, selects, documents and disposes of crime and criminals. It specifies both the nature of 'the crime problem' and what is being done about it. For this reason alone it is perhaps not surprising that it has been able to set the framework for the consideration of these matters. For this reason, too, its 'expert' personnel are far more likely to be called upon, and listened to, than 'armchair academics' from the social sciences theorising from 'the outside'.

A second reason is that it is much more convenient for ruling political groups to have 'the crime problem' circumscribed in this way; they are not likely to be well disposed to being told that their policies are criminogenic. Also, in societies where there is no major civil division and strife, there is likely to be sufficient commitment to the status quo to ensure that majority opinion is not favourably disposed to seeing crime in this way either. For the fact is, despite law-and-order scares and campaigns, political positions on crime control are rarely, if ever, decisive in determining election results. Consequently, efficient crime control is not usually the central consideration in determining the formulation of programmes of social, economic or political reform.

These factors usually conspire to ensure that if there *is* a political debate about crime control, it is a debate about the nature of, or reforms to, the criminal justice system. Politicians always add, at least as an aside, that their particular version of the 'good society' will ensure less crime than their opponents'. Once they are in power, however, and are therefore in the process of bringing about that good society, this can no longer be an issue. If the crime problem continues to exist, it can only be because of some inefficiency in the criminal justice system (which, of course, they inherited from their political predecessors).

Consequently, if the policies pursued by parties in power generate more and more crime, the outcome is likely to be more and more pressure and demands upon the criminal justice system, rather than a debate about the criminogenic qualities of those policies. Ultimately, this could lead to two outcomes, both of which challenge assumptions that I have made in developing the postclassical perspective: the limited significance ascribed to the criminal justice system in relation to controlling crime; and the clear distinction drawn between 'political' and 'criminal' activity.

First, the limited role ascribed to the criminal justice system only fully applies where that system is itself limited by the constraints of openness, accountability and the due process of law. When these constraints do not apply, the state's arrangements for arrest, detention, punishment and 'rehabilitation' can provide a much more potent means of control, as many totalitarian regimes bear witness. State control agencies such as police and courts can and do (as in the current law-and-order debates and legislation of the mid-1980s) portray themselves as hamstrung in their 'fight against crime' by 'unnecessary' restrictions of their powers. In a sense they are right; they are likely to be more successful without such constraints. The danger is that, where the 'crime problem' can be successfully defined as solely a criminal justice problem, regimes that pursue divisive, criminogenic policies may ultimately find themselves able to justify going outside the constraints of the due process of law. Given the factors, discussed above, that militate in favour of the 'crime problem' being successfully defined in this restricted way, the danger is a very real one.

However, divisive and criminogenic policies and the draconian and authoritarian criminal justice systems that they may generate are never likely to have things entirely their own way; for they also generate organised opposition. And this raises the second point – the relationship between 'political' and 'criminal' activity.

In Chapter 3 it was argued that Liebowitz and Horovitz (1968) had been a little premature in heralding the late 1960s as the beginning of an era of convergence between politics and crime. But their basic point holds good: only regimes that 'manage their affairs' reasonably well can impose a distinction. I take 'managing their affairs' to include not creating large-scale and organised groups of politically, economically or socially disaffected persons who do not feel that they have a stake in convention and are therefore prepared, collectively, to move outside it. In societies that do not manage their affairs well there may no longer be a consensus that violence and 'robbery' automatically constitute crime. For the ruling group, of course, they do. But outside of their circle there may be very widespread disagreement as to whether it constitutes crime or legitimate political activity. The current situation in Northern Ireland is perhaps to some extent illustrative of this situation (and it also illustrates the earlier point about the way in which ruling groups' continuing insistence on defining such activities as crime, and therefore solely a matter for the criminal justice system, can lead to the erosion of the usual principles of the due process of law).

Looked at another way, convergence could be taken as actually illustrating the point made earlier that crime is rarely a decisive political issue. For the point being made is that 'crime' only becomes such an issue when there is no longer general agreement that it *is* crime! It is not so much that crime and politics 'converge' when societies do not manage their affairs well (as Liebowitz and Horovitz, 1968, describe it), it is more that when they do not, there is a tendency for politics to *incorporate and redefine* 'crime'. Either way, however, these processes highlight a fundamental point about the postclassical conception of crime and its involvement in political processes: that crime is a shifting, situational and precarious human construct.

Perhaps the most important aim of the postclassical perspective is to relocate the issue of crime and its control into the social, political and economic context in which it belongs. The previous chapters have been an attempt to do that. Admittedly, they provide only a general and imprecise framework. However, since the issues are ultimately those of justice, equality and the good society it is, I hope, unsurprising and excusable that no definitive answers have been arrived at. The important point is that the debate on crime and its control is *about* these issues, and not simply about what is immediately politically and practically achievable.

Bibliography

American Friends Service Committee (1971), *Struggle for Justice*, New York: Hill and Wang.

Andenaes, J. (1974), *Punishment and Deterrence*, Ann Arbor: University of Michigan Press.

Anderson, E. (1976), 'The "Chivalrous" Treatment of the Female Offender in the Arms of the Criminal Justice System: a Review of the Literature', *Social Problems*, February.

Armstrong, G. and Wilson, M. (1973), 'City Politics and Deviancy Amplification' in I. Taylor and L. Taylor (eds), *Politics and Deviance*, Harmondsworth: Penguin.

Baldwin, J. (1974), 'Problem Housing Estates', *Journal of Social and Economic Administration*, Summer.

Baldwin, J. and Bottoms, A. (1976), *The Urban Criminal: A Study in Sheffield*, London: Tavistock.

Balkan, S., Berger, R. and Schmidt, J. (1980), *Crime and Deviance in America: A Critical Approach*, Belmont, CA: Wadsworth.

Bartrip, W. and Fenn, P. (1980), 'The Conventionalisation of Factory Crime: A Reassessment', *International Journal of the Sociology of Law*, May.

Bean, P. (1976), *Rehabilitation and Deviance*, London: Routledge and Kegan Paul.

Beccaria, C. (1963), *On Crimes and Punishments*, (translated by H. Paolucci), Indianapolis: Bobbs-Merrill (first published, as *Dei Delitti e delle Pene*, in 1764).

Becker, H. (1963), *Outsiders: Studies in the Sociology of Deviance*, New York: Free Press.

Becker, H. (1964), *The Other Side: Perspectives on Deviance*, New York: Free Press.

Bordua, D. (1961), 'Delinquent Subcultures: Sociological Interpretations of Gang Delinquency', *Annals of the American Academy of Political and Social Science*, November.

Bottomley, K. and Coleman, C. (1981), *Understanding Crime Rates*, London: Gower.

Bottoms, A. (1983), 'Neglected Features of Contemporary Penal Systems' in D. Garland and P. Young (eds), *The Power to Punish: Contemporary Penality and Social Analysis*, London: Heinemann.

Bottoms, A. and Mawby, R. (1987), 'A Localised Crime Survey in Contrasting Areas of a City', *British Journal of Criminology*, Spring.

Bowlby, J. (1946), *Forty-Four Juvenile Thieves*, London: Ballière, Tindall and Cox.

Box, S. (1971), *Deviance, Reality and Society*, London: Holt, Rinehart and Winston.

Box, S. (1981), *Deviance, Reality and Society*, London: Holt, Rinehart and Winston (2nd edn).

Box, S. (1987), *Recession, Crime and Punishment*, London: Macmillan.

Brake, M. (1980), *The Sociology of Youth Culture and Youth Subcultures*, London: Routledge and Kegan Paul.

Briar, S. and Piliavin, I. (1965), 'Delinquency, Situational Inducements and Commitment to Conformity', *Social Problems*, vol. 13.

Brody, S. (1976), *The Effectiveness of Sentencing: A Review of the Literature*, Home Office Research Report 35, London: HMSO.

Burgess, R. and Akers, R. (1966), 'A Differential Association-Reinforcement Theory of Criminal Behaviour', *Social Problems*, Fall.

Campbell, A. (1981), *Girl Delinquents*, Oxford: Blackwell.

Carson, W. (1970), 'White Collar Crime and the Enforcement of Factory Legislation' in W. Carson and P. Wiles (eds), *Crime and Delinquency in Britain*, London: Tavistock.

Centre for Contemporary Cultural Studies (1975), *Working Papers in Cultural Studies 7 and 8: Resistance through Rituals*, Birmingham: CCCS.

Cernkovich, S. and Giordano, P. (1987), 'Family Relationships and Delinquency', *Criminology*, May.

Christie, N. (1974), 'Utility and Social Values in Court Decisions on Punishment' in R. Hood (ed.), *Crime, Criminology and Public Policy*, London: Heinemann.

Cicourel, A. (1968), *The Social Organisation of Juvenile Justice*, New York: Wiley.

Cicourel, A. (1976), *The Social Organisation of Juvenile Justice* (2nd edition), London: Heinemann.

Clarke, R. (1980), 'Situational Crime Prevention: Theory and Practice', *British Journal of Criminology*, April.

Clemmer, D. (1958), *The Prison Community*, New York: Holt, Rinehart and Winston.

Clinard, M. (ed.) (1964), *Anomie and Deviant Behaviour*, Glencoe, IL: Free Press.

Clinard, M. (1978), *Cities with Little Crime: The Case of Switzerland*, Cambridge: Cambridge University Press.

Cloward, R. and Ohlin, L. (1960), *Delinquency and Opportunity: A Theory of Delinquent Gangs*, Chicago: Free Press.

Cloward, R. *et al.* (1960), *Theoretical Studies in the Social Organisation of the Prison*, New York: Social Science Research Council, Pamphlet 15.

Cohen, A. (1955), *Delinquent Boys: The Culture of the Gang*, Chicago: Free Press.

Cohen, R. (ed.) (1986), *Justice: Views from the Social Sciences*, New York: Plenum Press.

Cohen, S. (ed.) (1971), *Images of Deviance*, Harmondsworth: Penguin.

Cohen, S. (1985), *Visions of Social Control*, Cambridge: Polity Press.

Conger, R. (1976), 'Social Control and Learning Models of Delinquent Behaviour', *Criminology*, May.

Conrad, J. (1965), *Crime and its Correction: An International Survey of Attitudes and Practices*, London: Tavistock.

Cornish, D., and Clarke, R. (1986), *The Reasoning Criminal: Rational Choice Perspectives on Offending*, New York: Springer-Verlag.

Corrigan, P. and Frith, S. (1975), 'The Politics of Youth Culture', in Centre for Contemporary Cultural Studies, *Working Papers in Cultural Studies 7 and 8: Resistance through Rituals*, Birmingham: Centre for Contemporary Cultural Studies.

Cressey, D. (1953), *Other People's Money*, Chicago: Free Press.

Cressey, D. (ed.), (1961), *The Prison: Studies in Institutional Organisation and Change*, New York: Holt Rinehart and Winston.

Cressey, D. (1962), 'The Development of a Theory: Differential Association in E. Wolfgang,

L. Savitz and N. Johnston, *The Sociology of Crime and Delinquency*, New York: Wiley.

Downes, D. (1966), *The Delinquent Solution*, London: Routledge and Kegan Paul.

Downes, D. and Rock, P. (1982), *Understanding Deviance*, Oxford: Clarendon Press.

Durkheim, E. (1938), *The Rules of Sociological Method*, New York: Free Press of Glencoe.

Ehrlich, I. (1975), 'The Deterrent Effect of Capital Punishment: a Question of Life or Death', *American Economic Review*, vol. 65.

Ellis, L. (1982), 'Genetics and Criminal Behaviour', *Criminology*, May.

Erikson, K. (1966), *Wayward Puritans*, New York: Wiley.

European Committee on Crime Problems (1967), *The Effectiveness of Punishment and other Measures of Treatment*, Strasbourg: Council of Europe.

European Committee on Crime Problems (1972), *The Role of the School in the Prevention of Juvenile Delinquency*, Strasbourg: Council of Europe.

Eysenck, H. (1977), *Crime and Personality*, London: Paladin.

Farrington, D. (1972), 'Delinquency Begins at Home', *New Society*, 14 September.

Farrington, D. (1979), 'Longitudinal Research on Crime and Delinquency' in N. Morris and M. Tonry (eds), *Criminal Justice: An Annual Review of Research, Vol. 1*, Chicago and London: University of Chicago Press.

Farrington, D. and Morris, A. (1983), 'Sex, Sentencing and Reconviction', *British Journal of Criminology*, July.

Feldman, M. (1977), *Criminal Behaviour: A Psychological Analysis*, London: Wiley.

Ferri, E. (1967), *Criminal Sociology* (translated by J. Kelly and J. Lisle), New York: Agathon Press.

Finlayson, D. and Loughran, J. (1976), 'Pupils' Perceptions in High and Low Delinquency Schools', *Educational Research*, vol. 18.

Finnis, J. (1968), 'Old and New in Hart's Philosophy of Punishment', *Oxford Review*, vol. 8.

Finnis, J. (1980), *Natural Law and Natural Rights*, Oxford: Clarendon Press.

Fisher, C. and Mawby, R. (1982), 'Juvenile Delinquency and Police Discretion in an Inner City', *British Journal of Criminology*, January.

Fitzgerald, M. (1977), *Prisoners in Revolt*, Harmondsworth: Penguin.

Foucault, M. (1977), *Discipline and Punish*, Harmondsworth: Penguin.

Garland, D. (1985a), 'The Criminal and his Science', *British Journal of Criminology*, April.

Garland, D. (1985b), *Punishment and Welfare*, Aldershot: Gower.

Geis, G. and Stotland, E. (1980), *White Collar Crime: Theory and Research*, New York: Sage.

Giallombardo, R. (1966), *Society of Women*, New York: J. Wiley.

Giallombardo, R. (1974), *The Social World of Imprisoned Girls*, New York: J. Wiley.

Gibbs, J. (1975), *Crime, Punishment and Deterrence*, New York: Elsevier.

Gill, O. (1977), *Luke Street: Housing Policy, Conflict and the Creation of the Delinquency Area*, London: Macmillan.

Goffman, E. (1968a), *Stigma: Notes on the Management of Spoiled Identity*, Harmondsworth: Penguin.

Goffman, E. (1968b), *Asylums*, Harmondsworth: Penguin.

Graham, J. (1986), *Schools and Delinquency*, London: Home Office Research and Planning Unit.

Greenberg, D. (1979), 'Delinquency and the Age Structure of Society' in S. Messinger and E. Bittner (eds), *Criminology Review Yearbook*, Beverly Hills, CA: Sage

Hagan, J. (1987), *Modern Criminology: Crime, Criminal Behaviour and its Control*, New York: McGraw-Hill.

Halbasch, K. (1979), 'Differential Reinforcement Theory Examined', *Criminology*, August.

Hall, S., Critcher, C., Jefferson, T., Clarke, J., and Roberts, B. (1978), *Policing the Crisis: Mugging, the State and Law and Order*, London: Macmillan.
Hall Williams, J. (1982), *Criminology and Criminal Justice*, London: Butterworths.
Hammond, W. and Chayen, E. (1963), *Persistent Criminals*, London: HMSO.
Hargreaves, D. (1967), *Social Relations in a Secondary School*, London: Routledge and Kegan Paul.
Hart, H. L. A. (1983), *Essays on Bentham*, Oxford: Oxford University Press.
Hartl, E., Monnelly, E. and Elderkin, R. (1982), *Physique and Delinquent Behaviour: A Thirty Year Follow-Up of William H. Sheldon's Varieties of Delinquent Youth*, New York: Academic Press.
Heidensohn, F. (1985), *Women and Crime*, London: Macmillan.
Hindelang, M. (1972), 'The Relationship of Self-Reported Delinquency and Scales of the CPI and MMPI', *Journal of Criminal Law, Criminology and Police Science*, March.
Hindelang, M. (1973), 'Causes of Delinquency: a Partial Replication and Extension', *Social Problems*, Spring.
Hindelang, M. (1974), 'Moral Evaluations of Illegal Behaviours', *Social Problems*, no. 3.
Hirschi, T. (1969), *Causes of Delinquency*, Berkeley: University of California Press.
Hirschi, T. (1973), 'Procedural Rules and the Study of Deviant Behaviour', *Social Problems*.
Hirschi, T. (1986), 'On the Compatibility of Rational Choice and Social Control Theories of Crime' in D. Cornish and R. Clarke (eds), *The Reasoning Criminal: Rational Choice Perspectives on Offending*, New York: Springer-Verlag.
Hirschi, T. and Gottfredson, M. (1983), 'Age and the Explanation of Crime', *American Journal of Sociology*, no. 3.
Hirschi, T. and Gottfredson, M. (1986). 'The Distinction Between Crime and Criminality' in T. F. Hartnagel and R. A. Silverman (eds), *Critique and Explanation: Essays in Honour of Gwynne Nettler*, New Brunswick, NJ: Transaction.
Hirschi, T. and Hindelang, M. (1977), 'Intelligence and Delinquency: A Revisionist Review', *American Sociological Review*, vol. 42.
Hirst, P. (1975), 'Marx and Engels on Law, Crime and Morality' in I. Taylor, P. Walton and J. Young, *Critical Criminology*, London: Routledge and Kegan Paul.
Hood, R. (1978), 'Tolerance and the Tariff: Some Reflections on Fixing the Time Prisoners Serve in Custody' in J. Baldwin and A. Bottomley (eds), *Criminal Justice: Selected Readings*, London: Martin Robertson.
Hood, R. and Sparks, R. (1970), *Key Issues in Criminology*, London: Weidenfeld and Nicolson.
Hope, T. (1986), 'Crime, Community and Environment', *Journal of Environmental Psychology*, no. 6.
Hough, M. and Moxon, D. (1985), 'Dealing with Offenders: Popular Opinions and the Views of Victims', *Howard Journal*, August.
Ignatieff, M. (1978), *A Just Measure of Pain*, London: Macmillan.
Ignatieff, M. (1985), 'State, Civil Society and Total Institutions: a Critique of Recent Histories of Punishment' in S. Cohen and A. Scull (eds.), *Social Control and the State*, Oxford: Blackwell.
Jeffery, C. (1960), 'The Historical Development of Criminology' in H. Mannheim (ed.), *Pioneers in Criminology*, London: Stevens.
Jencks, C. (1987), 'Genes and Crime', *New York Review of Books*, 12 February.
Jenkins, P. (1984), 'Varieties of Enlightenment Criminology', *British Journal of Criminology*, April.

Jensen, G. and Eve, R. (1976), 'Sex Differences in Delinquency: An Examination of Popular Sociological Explanations', *Criminology*, February.

Jones, T., MacLean, B., and Young, J. (1986), *The Islington Crime Survey: Crime, Victimisation and Policing in Inner-City London*, Aldershot: Gower.

Kettle, M. (1984), 'The Police and the Left', *New Society*, vol. 70, no. 1146, 6 December, pp. 366–7.

Kneale, W. (1967), *The Responsibility of Criminals*, Oxford: Clarendon Press.

Koestler, A. (1970), *The Ghost in the Machine*, London: Pan.

Kornhauser, R. (1978), *Social Sources of Delinquency*, Chicago: University of Chicago Press.

La Fave, W. (1965), *Arrest, the Decision to Take a Suspect into Custody*, Boston: Little Brown.

Lambert, J. (1970), *Crime, Police and Race Relations*, Oxford: University Press.

Lander, B. (1954), *Towards an Understanding of Juvenile Delinquency*, New York: Columbia University Press.

Lea, J. and Young, J. (1984), *What Is to Be Done about Law and Order?*, Harmondsworth: Penguin.

Leigh, L. (ed.) (1980), *Economic Crime in Europe*, London: Macmillan.

Lemert, E. (1958), 'The Behaviour of the Systematic Check Forger', *Social Problems*, Fall.

Lemert, E. (1967), *Human Deviance, Social Problems and Social Control*, New York: Prentice Hall.

Lemert, E. (1974), 'Beyond Mead: the Societal Reaction to Deviance', *Social Problems*, vol. 21.

Liebowitz, M. and Horowitz, I. (1968), 'Social Deviance and Political Marginality: Towards a Redefinition of the Relationship between Sociology and Politics', *Social Problems*.

Lipton, D., Martinson, R., and Wilks, J. (1975), *The Effectiveness of Correctional Treatment: A Survey of Treatment Evaluation Studies*, New York: Praeger.

Mannheim, H. (ed.) (1960), *Pioneers in Criminology*, London: Stevens.

Mathieson, T. (1965), *The Defences of the Weak: A Sociological Study of a Norwegian Correctional Institution*, London: Tavistock.

Matthews, R. and Young, J. (eds) (1986), *Confronting Crime*, London: Sage.

Matza, D. (1964), *Delinquency and Drift*, New York: John Wiley.

Matza, D. (1969), *Becoming Deviant*, Englewood Cliffs, NJ: Prentice Hall.

Matza, D. and Sykes, G. (1957), 'Techniques of Neutralisation', *American Sociological Review*, December.

Matza, D. and Sykes, G. (1961), 'Juvenile Delinquency and Subterranean Values', *American Sociological Review*, October.

Mawby, R. (1977), 'Sexual Discrimination in the Law', *Probation Journal*.

Mawby, R. (1979), *Policing the City*, Farnborough: Saxon House.

Merton, R. (1938), 'Social Structure and Anomie', *American Sociological Review*, no. 3.

Monachesi, E. (1960), 'Cesare Beccaria' in H. Mannheim (ed.), *Pioneers in Criminology*, London: Stevens.

Morris, H. (1973), 'Persons and Punishment' in J. G. Murphy (ed.), *Punishment and Rehabilitation*, Belmont, CA: Wadsworth.

Morris, N. (1951), *The Habitual Criminal*, London: Longman.

Morris, T. and Morris, P. (1963), *Pentonville*, London: Routledge and Kegan Paul.

Newman, O. (1973), *Defensible Space*, London: Architectural Press.

Nieburg, H. (1974), 'Crime Prevention by Urban Design', *Society*, vol. 12.

Nozick, R. (1981), *Philosophical Explanations*, Oxford: Oxford University Press.

Nye, F. (1958), *Family Relationships and Delinquent Behaviour*, New York: J. Wiley.

Packer, H. (1968), *The Limits of the Criminal Sanction*, Stanford, CA: Stanford University Press.

Patrick, J. (1973), *A Glasgow Gang Observed*, London: Eyre Methuen.

Pearce, F. (1973), 'Crime, Corporations and the American Social Order' in I. Taylor and L. Taylor (eds.), *Politics and Deviance*, Harmondsworth: Penguin.

Pearson, G. (1975), *The Deviant Imagination*, London: Macmillan.

Pearson, G. (1976), 'Paki-Bashing in a North East Lancashire Cotton Town: A Case Study and its History' in G. Pearson and G. Mungham, *Working Class Youth Culture*, London: Routledge and Kegan Paul.

Phillipson, M. (1971), *Sociological Aspects of Crime and Delinquency*, London: Routledge and Kegan Paul.

Pitts, J. (1986), 'Black Young People and Juvenile Crime: Some Unanswered Questions' in R. Matthews and J. Young, *Confronting Crime*, London: Sage.

Quinney, R. (1975), 'Crime in a Capitalist Society: A Critical Philosophy of Legal Order' in I. Taylor, P. Walton and J. Young (eds), *Critical Criminology*, London, Routledge and Kegan Paul.

Radzinowicz, Sir Leon and Hood, R. (1986), *A History of English Criminal Law and its Administration from 1750. Vol. 5: The Emergence of Penal Policy*, London: Stevens.

Rathus, S. and Siegel, L. (1980), 'Crime and Personality Revisited', *Criminology*, August.

Rawls, J. (1972), *A Theory of Justice*, Oxford: Oxford University Press.

Riley, D. (1987), 'Parental Supervision Re-Examined?', *British Journal of Criminology*, Autumn.

Riley, D. and Shaw, M. (1985), *Parental Supervision and Juvenile Delinquency*, Home Office Research Study no. 83, London: HMSO.

Robins, D. and Cohen, P. (1978), *Knuckle Sandwich: Growing up in the Working-Class City*, Harmondsworth: Penguin.

Rodman, H. and Grams, P. (1967), 'Family and Delinquency', prepared for the US President's Commission on Law Enforcement and Administration of Justice: Task Force Report on Juvenile Delinquency and Youth Crime.

Roshier, B. (1977), 'The Function of Crime Myth', *Sociological Review*, May.

Roshier, B. and Teff, H. (1980), *Law and Society in England*, London: Tavistock.

Rowe, A. and Tittle, C. (1977), 'Life-Cycle Changes and Criminal Propensity', *Sociological Quarterly*.

Rutter, M. and Giller, H. (1983), *Juvenile Delinquency: Trends and Perspectives*, Harmondsworth: Penguin.

Rutter, M., Maughan, B., Mortimore, P., Ouston, J. with Smith, A. (1979), *Fifteen Thousand Hours: Secondary Schools and their Effects on Children*, London: Open Books.

Schuessler, K. and Cressey, D. (1950), 'Personality Characteristics of Criminals', *American Journal of Sociology*, vol. 55.

Schur, E. (1973), *Radical Non-intervention*, Englewood Cliffs, NJ: Prentice Hall.

Shaw, C. (1929), *Delinquency Areas*, Chicago: University of Chicago Press.

Shaw, C. and McKay, H. (1942), *Juvenile Delinquency and Urban Areas*, Chicago: University of Chicago Press.

Short, J. and Strodtbeck, F. (1965), *Group Process and Gang Delinquency*, Chicago: Chicago University Press.

Smith, R. (1962), 'The Incredible Electrical Conspiracy' in M. Wolfgang, L. Savitz and N. Johnston (eds), *The Sociology of Crime and Delinquency*, New York: Wiley.

Stevens, P. and Willis, C. (1979), *Race, Crime and Arrests*, Home Office Research Study no. 58, London: HMSO.

Sutherland, E. (1945), 'Is White Collar Crime Crime?', *American Sociological Review*.

Sutherland, E. and Cressey, D. (1970), *Principles of Criminology*, Philadelphia: Lippincott.

Sykes, G. (1958), *The Society of Captives*, Princeton, NJ: Princeton University Press.

Taft, D. (1942), *Criminology*, New York: Macmillan.

Taylor, I. and Taylor, L. (eds) (1973), *Politics and Deviance*, Harmondsworth: Penguin.

Taylor, I., Walton, P. and Young, J. (1973), *The New Criminology*, London: Routledge and Kegan Paul.

Taylor, I., Walton, P. and Young, J. (eds) (1975), *Critical Criminology*, London: Routledge and Kegan Paul.

Taylor, L. (1971), *Deviance and Society*, London: Nelson.

Taylor, L., Lacey, R. and Bracken, D. (1980), *In Whose Best Interests? The Unjust Treatment of Children in Courts and Institutions*, London: Cobden Trust.

Ten, C. (1987), *Crime, Guilt and Punishment: A Philosophical Introduction*, Oxford: Clarendon Press.

Thomas, W. I. (1923), *The Unadjusted Girl*, Montclair, NJ: Patterson Smith (1969 reprint).

Thrasher, F. (1927), *The Gang*, Chicago: University of Chicago Press.

Tierney, J. (1988), 'Viewpoint – Romantic Fictions: the Re-emergence of the Crime as Politics Debate', *Sociological Review*, February.

Twining, W. and Twining, P. (1973), 'Bentham on Torture', *Northern Ireland Legal Quarterly*, vol. 24, no. 3.

Van Den Haag, E. (1975), *Punishing Criminals*, New York: Basic Books.

Veblen, T. (1922), *Theory of the Leisure Class*, London: Macmillan.

Vold, G. (1958), *Theoretical Criminology*, New York: Oxford University Press.

Vold, G. and Bernard, T. (1986), *Theoretical Criminology*, Oxford: Oxford University Press.

Von Hirsch, A. (1983), '"Neoclassicism," Proportionality, and the Rationale for Punishment: Thoughts on the Scandinavian Debate', *Crime and Delinquency*, January.

Walker, N. (1981), 'Feminist Extravaganzas', *Criminal Law Review*, June.

Walker, N. (1985), *Sentencing: Theory, Law and Practice*, London: Butterworths.

West, D. (1963), *The Habitual Prisoner*, London: Macmillan.

West, D. (1969), *Present Conduct and Future Delinquency*, London: Heinemann.

West, D., and Farrington, D. (1973), *Who Becomes Delinquent?*, London: Heinemann.

Whymant, R. (1975), 'The Friendly Neighbourhood Police State', *The Guardian*, 5 September.

Wiatrowski, M., Griswold, D. and Roberts, M. (1981), 'Social Control Theory and Delinquency', *American Sociological Review*.

Wilkins, L. (1964), *Social Deviance: Social Policy, Action and Research*, London: Tavistock.

Wilson, H. (1987), 'Parental Supervision Re-Examined', *British Journal of Criminology*, Summer.

Wilson, J. (1975), *Thinking about Crime*, New York: Vintage.

Wilson, J. and Herrnstein, R. (1985), *Crime and Human Nature*, New York: Simon and Schuster.

Wolfgang, M. (1960), 'Cesare Lombroso' in H. Mannheim, (ed.), *Pioneers in Criminology*, London: Stevens.

Wright, M. (1982), *Making Good: Prisons, Punishment and Beyond*, London: Hutchinson.

Yablonsky, L. (1962), *The Violent Gang*, New York: Macmillan.

Young, J. (1971), 'The Role of the Police as Amplifiers of Deviancy' in S. Cohen (ed.), *Images of Deviance*, Harmondsworth: Penguin.

Young, J. (1986), 'The Failure of Criminology: the Need for a Radical Realism' in R. Matthews and J. Young (eds), *Confronting Crime*, London: Sage.

Zimring, F. and Hawkins, G. (1973), *Deterrence: the Legal Threat in Crime Control*, Chicago: University of Chicago Press.

Index